YORK NOTES

Twelfth Night

William Shakespeare

Note by Emma Smith

Longman

York Press

YORK PRESS
322 Old Brompton Road, London SW5 9JH

PEARSON EDUCATION LIMITED
Edinburgh Gate, Harlow,
Essex CM20 2JE, United Kingdom
Associated companies, branches and representatives throughout the world

First published 2001

ISBN 0-582-43150-6

Designed by Vicki Pacey
Phototypeset by Gem Graphics, Trenance, Mawgan Porth, Cornwall
Colour reproduction and film output by Spectrum Colour
Produced by Pearson Education North Asia Limited, Hong Kong

SA013604

CONTENTS

PART ONE

INTRODUCTION

HOW TO STUDY A PLAY

Studying on your own requires self-discipline and a carefully thought-out work plan in order to be effective.

- Drama is a special kind of writing (the technical term is 'genre') because it needs a performance in the theatre to arrive at a full interpretation of its meaning. Try to imagine that you are a member of the audience when reading the play. Think about how it could be presented on the stage, not just about the words on the page.

- Drama is often about conflict of some sort (which may be below the surface). Identify the conflicts in the play and you will be close to identifying the large ideas or themes which bind all the parts together.

- Make careful notes on themes, character, plot and any subplots of the play

- Why do you like or dislike the characters in the play? How do your feelings towards them develop and change?

- Playwrights find nonrealistic ways of allowing an audience to see into the minds and motives of their characters, for example **soliloquy, aside** or music. Consider how such dramatic devices are used in the play you are studying.

- Think of the playwright writing the play. Why were these particular arrangements of events, characters and speeches chosen?

- Cite exact sources for all quotations, whether from the text itself or from critical commentaries. Wherever possible find your own examples from the play to back up your own opinions.

- Always express your ideas in your own words.

This York Note offers an introduction to *Twelfth Night* and cannot substitute for close reading of the text and the study of secondary sources.

A recent edition of the American tabloid talk-show hosted by Jerry Springer was entitled 'My boyfriend is a girl', and featured women who maintained they had been unaware that their dates were not male after all. Part of *Twelfth Night*'s appeal is to the same slightly prurient interest in girls dressed as boys and the erotic games this seems to involve. If the classic romantic comedy could be summarised as girl meets boy and falls in love, *Twelfth Night* offers a beguiling range of variations on this theme: girl falls in love with girl dressed as boy, boy falls for girl dressed as boy, girl dressed as boy makes herself attractive to girl and boy. What this shows is that these titillating combinations are not just a modern peccadillo, but that the ongoing interest in gender roles, cross-dressing and sexuality as seen in films from *Some Like It Hot* via *Tootsie* and *Mrs Doubtfire* to *The Crying Game* is preempted by Shakespeare in his comedy *Twelfth Night*. In this context, the play's subtitle 'What You Will', becomes laden with innuendo, a version of 'anything goes' or 'whatever turns you on'.

The play is, of course, much more than this. It shows a number of instances of love, from selfless to selfish, from altruistic to narcissistic. It is concerned with unrequited and unexpected love. It also has a vein of cruelty in which the audience is uncomfortably implicated. There is a hectic, slightly desperate feeling about the action, as if the characters are running out of options, hence the hurry to get married and wrap everything up at the end. It is a comedy with a melancholy aftertaste, a temporary umbrella against the wintry rain that Feste sings of in his final song, and so it is perhaps not surprising that *Twelfth Night* is often identified as Shakespeare's last comedy, shading into the darker mood of the so-called 'problem plays' and the great tragedies. Reading *Twelfth Night*, one of Shakespeare's most popular plays, provokes a combination of different responses, as the representatives of order and misrule battle it out for final supremacy in a story named after the last day of the Christmas festivities.

PART TWO

Summaries & Commentaries

Twelfth Night was first printed in 1623, seven years after Shakespeare's death in 1616, as part of the first collected edition of his works, *Mr William Shakespeares Comedies, Tragedies, & Histories*, known as the First Folio. In the contents page of this edition it is listed under 'Comedies' and given its full title 'Twelfth Night, or What You Will'. All modern editions of the play, including the New Penguin text edited by M.M. Mahood to which this Note will refer, are derived from this first publication (see Background, on The Texts of Shakespeare's Plays). *Twelfth Night* was probably written in late 1600–1, and had its first performance in 1601. Attempts to suggest it was premiered at Elizabeth's court on twelfth night in 1601 are fanciful (see Themes, on Twelfth Night), although Shakespeare may have taken the name of his lovesick Duke from Elizabeth's Italian guest on that occasion, the young nobleman Don Virginio Orsino, Duke of Bracchiano. We do know that it was performed at the Middle Temple in February 1602, the feast of Candlemas, because a law student John Manningham wrote in his diary:

> At our feast we had a play called *Twelfth Night, or What You Will*, much like *The Comedy of Errors* or *Menaechmi* in Plautus, but most like and near to that in Italian called *Inganni* [see Background, on Literary Background]. A good practice in it to make the steward believe his lady widow was in love with him, by counterfeiting a letter as from his lady, in general terms telling him what she liked best in him, and prescribing his gesture in smiling, his apparel, etc., and then when he came to practise, making him believe they took him to be mad.

Manningham's account is interesting in its exclusive stress on the Malvolio plot, giving an indication of what one early spectator found most engaging about the play (see Critical History & Broader Perspectives).

Viola is shipwrecked on the coast of Illyria, in a storm which she believes has drowned her twin brother Sebastian. Disguising herself in male clothes, she goes to work for the Duke Orsino as a page. Orsino is in love with Olivia, who does not return his affections and is in long mourning for her dead brother. Viola, who has taken the name Cesario, becomes a firm favourite with Orsino who sends his young page as an emissary to Olivia. Olivia entertains Cesario, and quickly falls in love with him/her. The situation is complicated by Viola's own love for Orsino.

Meanwhile, Olivia's drunken uncle Sir Toby Belch, her lady-in-waiting Maria and her would-be suitor Sir Andrew Aguecheek, together with her servant Fabian and fool Feste, have hatched a plot against her puritanical steward Malvolio, who interrupted their late-night carousing. Maria fakes Olivia's handwriting in a letter to Malvolio which tells him his mistress is in love with him, and that she wishes him always to smile and to wear yellow stockings and cross-garters. Malvolio falls for the trick, and follows the instructions. Olivia thinks him mad and her household continue the 'jest' by imprisoning him as a lunatic, where Feste pretends to be a priest to torment him.

It emerges, unbeknown to Viola, that Sebastian has been rescued by a sailor named Antonio, who has strong feelings for him. Antonio is arrested for an old offence against the Illyrian state, and mistakes Viola for Sebastian when asking for help. Sebastian himself is mistaken for Viola when he becomes embroiled in a duel Sir Toby is encouraging Andrew to fight against Cesario for the hand of Olivia. Olivia too mistakes Sebastian for Cesario; Sebastian is attracted to her and they are swiftly married. In the final scene, all is revealed. Orsino agrees to marry Viola, to join Olivia and Sebastian. Sir Toby is to marry Maria. Sir Andrew and Antonio are left out of this resolution, as is Malvolio, who vows revenge on his tormentors. The play ends with Feste's song.

Act I

SCENE 1 **Orsino, Duke of Illyria, expresses his deep love for Olivia, seeming to enjoy the sensations of unrequited romance. Valentine returns from Olivia's household where Orsino's courtship has been rejected, as Olivia is in mourning for her dead brother**

The play opens with Orsino's lovesick musing. His first speech is preoccupied with the condition of being in love, and when Curio, one of his attendants, suggests the distraction of hunting, this too operates as a **metaphor** for love in the popular Elizabethan **pun** on hart (deer)/heart. Valentine's news from his embassy to Olivia is not promising. She has devoted herself to a nun-like existence in memory of her dead brother, and the mourning period is to last seven years. Orsino turns this into praise for her constancy and her capacity to love, and looks forward to the day when this love will be devoted to him.

Orsino's language through the scene is characterised by excess, and thus introduces this important theme into the play (see Themes, on Excess). Like the young Romeo who is in love with Rosaline before he sees Juliet in the earlier play *Romeo and Juliet*, there is a suggestion in the **hyperbole** of his language that he is in love with the sensation of being in love, rather than with a particular woman. This suggestion may be strengthened by the fact that he does not mention Olivia by name until line 20. His love is discussed in terms of appetite – another important theme of the play. Orsino's first scene is important in establishing the status of his love for Olivia, and it seems as if it is a rather self-indulgent emotion which has rather little to do with her as an individual and instead rests on an idealised image of her 'purg[ing] the air of pestilence' (line 21). Orsino's love at first sight (line 22) also suggests a romanticised view of Olivia (see Characterisation), and his language in this scene is often conventional, even clichéd, influenced by the vogue for love **sonnets** following the popularity of the Italian poet **Petrarch** and those English writers influenced by him, including Shakespeare himself. Another interpretation, however, is that his language indicates his capacity for strong feeling and a responsiveness to music, often a positive aspect of Shakespeare's characterisation. What might be criticised as extravagance could be more charitably interpreted as expansiveness, a zest and vigour for life's pleasures (see Characterisation). That this is not only, or primarily, a romantic, spiritual form of love is stressed by the vivid image (lines 22–4) of his consuming physical desires, 'like fell and cruel hounds': the reference is to the legend of Actaeon, a huntsman who was turned into a deer and torn to pieces by his own hounds as a punishment for glimpsing the virginal goddess Diana bathing.

In this love-soaked atmosphere, it is highly appropriate that the go-between for Orsino and Olivia should be called Valentine. Our first impressions of Olivia, via this report, also identify her as a character of strong, even excessive emotions (see Themes, on Excess, and Characterisation). While she and Orsino are opposites, we might think that they are rather similar, single-minded personalities. The length of her mourning for her brother, the severity of her veiled demeanour and her continual weeping – 'And water once a day her chamber round / With eye-offending brine' (lines 30–1) – all suggest a woman of intense passions. Valentine's language suggests that she is a too-rigid observer of mourning rituals. In establishing two such extreme characters, the play arouses our curiosity and interest about how events will unfold.

4 **dying fall** musical cadence which falls to its resolution

9 **quick** keen

12 **pitch** height, excellence

15 **high fantastical** extremely imaginative

18 **hart** deer, with a pun on 'heart'

23 **fell** savage

27 **element** sky

28 **ample** full

29 **cloistress** nun

31 **season** preserve

34 **frame** construction

36 **shaft** Cupid's arrow

38 **liver, brain, and heart** Renaissance thought held these organs to be the centre of the passions, judgements and sentiments

40 **self** sole

SCENE *2*   **Viola, having survived a shipwreck in which her brother is feared drowned, is cast up on the Illyrian coast with the captain. The captain knows of Orsino's love for Olivia, Viola has heard her father mention Orsino, and she hears of Orsino's unrequited suit. Viola decides to dress as a eunuch and enter Orsino's service**

Viola discovers through questioning the captain that she has landed in Illyria, and hears about its prominent residents Orsino and Olivia. She expresses the hope that her brother has been saved from drowning, and the Captain encourages her in this apparently forlorn wish. We learn that Olivia is in mourning not only for her brother but for her father who has also recently died. Viola takes the quick decision to dress in male clothing and to present herself as a servant to Orsino.

> Viola's arrival by water literalises two images from the previous scene: the sea of love in Orsino's first speech (line 11), and Olivia's saltwater tears or 'brine' (line 31), and thus her mediating role between them is subtly suggested. She also shares with Olivia the loss of a brother, and this sense of emotional identification may explain her exclamation 'O, that I served that lady' (line 42). Her brisk question, 'What country, friends, is this?' (line 1) suggests that she is resourceful, thinking about their situation and what is to be done rather than succumbing to fatigue or despair or grief. In this she is immediately contrasted with our initial image of Orsino and Olivia, both of whom are presented as static, passively responding rather than actively instigating. Viola's decision to dress herself as a eunuch is not immediately comprehensible. There may be a hint at her compatibility with Orsino in her abilities in music – the comfort he demands at the beginning of the play. But questions remain. If her father knew Orsino, why does she not ask for the Duke's hospitality after her ordeal? Why does she not tell of her 'estate' (line 45) – both social and emotional – and gain a welcome proper to her status? Rather, Viola chooses 'disguise' and to 'conceal'. This

unusual response might be explained with reference to her emotional distress after her suffering. Perhaps, following the trauma of the shipwreck and her delivery into a strange country, she is not thinking straight. In Trevor Nunn's film of the play, a prologue tells us that Messaline, the country of Viola's birth, is at war with Illyria, a name associated with doom. Illyria is immediately represented as a sinister police state, and it is clear that Viola's actions are motivated by fear, as she and her fellow survivors flee into some caves in the cliff when a menacing squad of black-uniformed horsemen gallop along the beach. Whatever the reason, Viola adopts male attire as some kind of physical, social or psychological protection, just as previous Shakespearean heroines such as Rosalind in *As You Like It* and Julia in *The Two Gentlemen of Verona* had done before.

2 **Illyria** on the Adriatic coast, roughly equivalent to the former Yugoslavia

4 **Elysium** the heaven of classical mythology

5 **Perchance** perhaps

6 **perchance** here the pun plays on the previous sense, and means 'only by chance'

11 **driving** being driven (by the wind)

15 **Arion** a Greek musician who, according to mythology, was saved from the sea by a dolphin enchanted by his singing

19–21 **Mine own ... of him** my own escape, and your story, give me hope that he, too, has been saved

32 **murmur** rumour

43 **delivered** revealed

45 **estate** status
    compass achieve

48 **behaviour** outward appearance

52 **character** appearance and behaviour

55 **become** be fitting for

56 **The form of my intent** what I intend

57 **eunuch** castrated male

61 **hap** happen, come about by chance

62 **wit** plan, design

63 **mute** eunuchs in oriental harems were often attended by mutes

SCENE 3   Sir Toby Belch, uncle to Olivia, discusses his niece's
behaviour with her attendant, Maria, who advises him to
keep his revelry under control. Sir Toby's companion Sir
Andrew Aguecheek enters and his vanity and literal-
mindedness is made the butt of the others' quick wits

This scene introduces the characters who will bear the burden of the
play's comedy, and, as is usual in Shakespearean drama, it is in prose
rather than the **blank verse** of the previous two scenes. Maria and Sir
Toby discuss, in bantering and sometimes bawdy style, the behaviour of
the knights and Olivia's displeasure at their 'ill hours' (line 5) and at the
introduction of Aguecheek as a potential suitor. Aguecheek is clearly
wealthy and claims to be well educated, but, as Maria says, 'a very fool'
(line 22), and this diagnosis is confirmed when he fails to understand Sir
Toby's encouragement 'accost', and takes it for Maria's name. He vows to
remain at Olivia's house to try and promote his wooing of her, although
has not had much encouragement. Their dedication to enjoyment
and to 'revels' is made clear as they go off in a 'caper' to continue their
festivities.

> Like Orsino and Olivia in the first scene, Sir Toby is characterised
> by excess (see Themes, on Excess). He roundly refuses Maria's
> sensible remark about self-restraint: 'you must confine yourself
> within the modest limits of order' (lines 7–8). His is a character
> devoted to self-gratification and without much thought for
> others, but he is not the only character in the play who could be
> so described (see Themes, on Love & Self-love). Sir Toby's
> motivations are selfish, fleshly ones. He lives to enjoy drinking
> and merrymaking, and can be seen as the embodiment of the play's
> festive comic energies (see Themes, on Twelfth Night). He and Sir
> Andrew, often played as a comic double act of fat man/thin man are
> popular with audiences as a bawdy, earthy contrast to the elevated
> emotions and expressions of the two noble households of Orsino
> and Olivia.

6 **except before excepted** a legalism, meaning to exclude what has already
been excluded

8 **modest limits of order** bounds of reasonable behaviour

11 **an** if

18 **tall** courageous (as well as of height)

20 **three thousand ducats** intended to register that Sir Andrew has a substantial income

21 **have but ... ducats** he'll spend the lot in a year

22 **very** complete

25 **without book** by memory

26 **natural** foolish

28 **gust** relish

31–2 **substractors** detractors

37 **coistrel** knave, low person

39 **parish top** spinning top

Castiliano, *vulgo* a much-discussed phrase, with 'Speak of the devil' probably its nearest equivalent

44 **shrew** probably a reference to Maria's small size, but the other association of shrew – as ill-tempered woman – means it is hardly complimentary

46 **Accost** a naval term, meaning to go alongside

47 **chambermaid** lady-in-waiting

62 **in hand** to deal with

64 **Marry** mild oath, originally 'By Mary'

66 **Thought is free** a stock response to the question 'Do you think I'm a fool?'

67 **buttery bar** serving counter in a liquor store-room. Most performances make this a reference to Maria's breasts

70 **dry** thirsty, perhaps with an association of 'withered' or impotent

72 **keep my hand dry** 'Fools have wit enough to keep themselves out of the rain' was a proverb

73 **dry** both 'not wet' and 'ironic'

77 **canary** sweet wine

82 **eater of beef** referring to the belief that beef dulled the mind, as in the insult 'beef-witted' in *Troilus and Cressida* (II.1.13).

87 ***Pourquoi?*** (French) 'why?'

89 **tongues** pronounced in the same way as curling 'tongs', hence the following pun on hair styling

98 **huswife** housewife and prostitute. The joke is about venereal disease, which was thought to cause baldness

109 **kickshawses** trifles, worthless knick-knacks

111 **betters** social superiors

112 **old man** experienced person, but perhaps with a reference to Sir Toby's age

113 **galliard** a lively dance-step

114 **caper** pun on 'dance' and 'spice' for cooking mutton

116 **back-trick** innuendo, referring to reverse steps in the dance but with sexual connotations perhaps following on from 'mutton', slang term for a prostitute

120 **Mistress Mall's picture** pictures were often protected by curtains, though this may be a specific reference to a contemporary scandal about one of Elizabeth I's maids of honour, Mary Fitton, who was disgraced after giving birth to the Earl of Pembroke's illegitimate child in 1601

122 **coranto** a fast dance

123 **sink-apace** anglicised version of the French 'cinquepas', a dance like a galliard

128 **dun-coloured stock** brown stockings (this is a textual crux which is differently rendered in different editions. See Literary Background, on The Texts of Shakespeare's Plays)

130 **Taurus** astrological signs were thought to govern particular parts of the body

SCENE 4   **The discussion between Valentine and Viola dressed in male clothing indicates that her introduction to Orsino has gone well and that she is already in his confidence. Orsino then despatches Viola (called Cesario in her male disguise) to Olivia to woo her in his stead, but Viola's final aside reveals that she is herself in love with Orsino**

Clearly the relationship between Orsino and Viola/Cesario has made good progress over the intervening days since her decision of I.2, and Valentine comments on the rapidity with which the new servant has been accepted. Orsino confirms this intimacy: 'I have unclasped / To thee the book even of my secret soul' (lines 13–14), and asks his trusted servant to go to Olivia and wait until she admits this courier of Orsino's love. Viola is not confident that she can gain entrance, but Orsino urges her to 'leap all civil bounds' (line 21) and do anything necessary to gain an audience with Olivia. He thinks that Viola's feminine looks will persuade Olivia where others have failed, suggesting that Viola's male disguise is not entirely successful when 'all is semblative a woman's part' (line 34). In her disguise as Cesario, Viola seems to combine the physical qualities of both male and female (see Themes, on Gender). Orsino promises great fortune to Viola if she succeeds: 'And thou shalt live as freely as thy lord, / To call his fortunes thine' (lines 39–40). Viola's own final couplet, an **aside** to the audience, reveals that Orsino's quick intimacy is reciprocated, and that she is in the uncomfortable position of wooing a woman as a wife for a man she herself is determined to marry: 'Whoe'er I woo, myself would be his wife' (line 42).

This is an important scene for moving the plot forward, and Viola's rapid discovery that she loves Orsino may give a retrospective explanation to her initial decision to go to his household in I.2. Orsino, too, has been able to confide in his new servant, and has clearly formed a trusting attachment to Cesario. The simple admission of their intimacy in lines 13–14 is in sharp contrast to the elevated diction of his professions of love for Olivia in the first scene. Their compatibility, the companionship on which their ultimate marriage will be founded, is thus immediately established, and by choosing not to show us the early scenes of this relationship, Shakespeare presents it to us at this point as quickly, but solidly begun.

The **dramatic irony** of Orsino's speech on Cesario's femininity (lines 30–40) establishes the gender confusion which is to become increasingly important to the plot's comic complications (see Themes, on Gender). There's **irony**, too, in Orsino's promise of shared fortunes if Viola is successful in gaining Olivia for him. Sharing in Orsino's life, in his fortunes both material and circumstantial, is exactly what Viola is aiming at, but through marrying Orsino herself rather than securing him another wife.

5 **his humour** his changeability

12 **aloof** apart

13 **unclasped** ornate books were often fastened together with clasps

15 **address thy gait** direct your steps

17 **grow** take root

28 **nuncio** messenger

    aspect appearance

32 **rubious** ruby-red

    pipe voice

34 **semblative** resembles

part role (referring to the fact that women's roles were taken by male
actors)
35 **constellation** character as decided by the stars
41 **barful strife** inner struggle

SCENE 5   Set in Olivia's household, this scene introduces the
characters of Olivia herself, her steward Malvolio and
Feste, the clown. Feste tries to jest Olivia out of her
melancholy, and Malvolio expresses his disapproval of the
clown. Viola arrives on Orsino's behalf, and is granted an
audience with Olivia. During their private conversation in
which Viola tells her of Orsino's love, it seems that Olivia
is falling in love with the messenger (whom she believes to
be a man). She sends Malvolio after Viola to give her a
ring

At Feste's introduction, we are told that he has been absent for some
unspecified period, and Maria tells him that Olivia will scold him for this.
His jesting, glancing speech refuses to take this threat seriously, and this
demeanour continues when Olivia enters with Malvolio and her other
attendants. She and Feste engage in a series of jokes as he tries to cheer
her up, asking her why she weeps for her brother if she believes him to be
in heaven (lines 61–7), suggesting that it is she who is the 'fool', not he.
When asked his opinion, Malvolio is highly critical, wondering why
Olivia 'takes delight in such a barren rascal' (lines 78–9); for her
part, Olivia diagnoses this response as Malvolio being 'sick of self-love'
(line 85), and defends the particular position of the paid fool to speak his
mind: 'There is no slander in an allowed fool' (lines 88–9).

News comes that a 'young gentleman' (line 94) has come from
Orsino's household to speak with her, and that 'he' is being entertained
by Sir Toby at the gate. Olivia sends Malvolio to dismiss the visitor, and
Sir Toby, apparently drunk – he mishears 'lethargy' as 'lechery', for
example – reels in. Malvolio returns to report that the visitor is persistent
and will not be dismissed, and Olivia asks questions about the appearance
of this emissary. Malvolio reports that he is between childhood and
maturity – 'standing water between boy and man' (line 154) – and
something in this description causes Olivia to relent. She puts on her veil

to receive her visitor. It may be the veils that cause Viola to deliver the apparent insult, to a noblewoman and her attendants, of being unable to distinguish the mistress of the house (line 162), but this bold, almost pert approach is characteristic of Viola's behaviour in the rest of the scene. She alternates between apparently prepared **eulogy** – 'Most radiant, exquisite, and unmatchable beauty' (line 163) – and the deflating commentary of 'I would be loath to cast away my speech' (line 166) if she is not addressing it to the right woman. Viola makes a number of references to her 'speech' (lines 166, 174, 183), making clear it is a prepared script rather than spontaneous and heartfelt. Olivia seems both drawn to and irritated by this chirpy delivery, maintaining that ''Tis not that time of moon with me, to make one in so skipping a dialogue' (lines 192–3), while at the same time exchanging wordplay and agreeing to a private conference with the young man.

When Olivia and Viola are alone together, Orsino's suit is pursued more directly. Olivia asks questions about Orsino's love, to which Viola replies in persuasive terms. It is clear, though, that it is less the master and more the servant who interests Olivia, who begins to ask questions of Viola's 'parentage' (line 266). Olivia repeats that she 'cannot love' Orsino (line 269), and says he must not send any further message to her 'Unless, perchance, you come to me again / To tell me how he takes it' (lines 270–1).When Viola leaves, refusing to be paid and asking for 'recompense' to her master instead (line 274), Olivia has a brief **soliloquy** which reveals that she has fallen in love like catching the plague, and that she intends to 'let it be' (line 287). She commands Malvolio to follow after Viola and give her a ring, under the pretext that Viola left the ring with her. Malvolio is also told to tell Viola to return the next day to hear the 'reasons' why she cannot accept Orsino. In her final soliloquy, Olivia confirms her intention to leave the matter in the hands of fate: 'What is decreed must be, and be this so' (line 302).

The beginning of the scene is in prose, as Maria and Feste discuss his absence. Lines 24–6 may suggest that Feste foresees the marriage between Sir Toby and Maria, and, if so, it is an early indication of his ability to see more in situations than other people (see Characterisation). Olivia has been mentioned in each of the three preceding scenes: now we see her for the first time, and the impression does not entirely accord with the accounts we have been given of her. Rather than being a 'cloistress' (I.1.29), she seems a capable head of her household, engaging in wordplay with her fool, delivering her opinion of Malvolio and of her kinsman Sir Toby, and apparently enjoying her interview with Viola. At Olivia's entrance, she maintains the relaxed rhythms of prose: she clearly does not stand on ceremony in contrast to Valentine's image of her incarcerated by a crippling ritual of mourning (I.1). She enjoys an easygoing relationship with Feste, and speaks lightly, perhaps jokingly, to Malvolio. Some productions use the contrast between the view of Olivia from Orsino's household with what we see in this scene to suggest that in fact her mourning has been a smokescreen to deter Orsino's unwelcome advances; others, to suggest a more complicated picture than the goddess of Orsino's desires.

Olivia's analysis of Malvolio's 'self-love' (line 85) is another early indication of how the plot will unfold, but it can be related to Viola's shrewd observation of Olivia herself later in the scene: 'you are too proud' (line 239). Malvolio is only the most extreme version of a type we keep encountering in the play, as a kind of narcissism preoccupies many of its main protagonists. The Royal Shakespeare Company production of the play directed by Peter Gill in 1974 made this point clear by having the stage dominated by a huge mural of the classical Narcissus, who fell in love with his own reflection and so became a prototype of the self-obsessed individual (see Themes, on Love & Self-love). This first introduction to Malvolio identifies him as a killjoy: unlike his mistress, he can take no pleasure in Feste's wit, and his disapproval is cold and cutting. Trevor Nunn's film made it clear, through showing Feste's implacable stare at Malvolio, that this scene foreshadows the hostility between the two which will have its open expression in IV.2.

The scene is characterised throughout by dialogue, by a back-and-forth kind of conversation which speaks of relaxed social relations. This relaxation comes close to intimacy in the long exchange between Viola and Olivia (discussed in more detail in Textual Analysis, Text 1). Viola uses the imagery of theatre simultaneously to advance and to undermine her message of Orsino's love. She talks of playing 'a part' (line 172), admits that 'I am not that I play', and mentions the speech she must deliver as if it were a script she has learned: 'I took great pains to study it, and 'tis poetical' (line 197). The developing intimacy between the two is revealed as Olivia echoes this imagery: 'You are now out of your text' (line 222), i.e. you are going beyond your scripted lines. She takes up the task of deflating high-blown love **rhetoric**, reducing the conventional poetic device known as the **blazon**, in which the lover's eyes, lips, cheeks, hair etc. were all separately discussed in clichéd terms, to a **bathetic** catalogue: 'as, item: two lips, indifferent red; item, two grey eyes, with lids to them' (lines 236–7). Viola is not quite disrespectful, but almost. Something of this unpompous, rather maverick treatment of her mistress seems to be what attracts Olivia to her. It can be seen that the energy and spontaneity of Viola's witty remarks are much more charismatic than the rather flowery and impersonal language of Orsino's passions in I.1, and it is presumably these which prompt Olivia to grant the unprecedented private meeting with this attractive young messenger.

Viola's speech is extremely persuasive, and the 'make me a willow cabin at your gate' is a powerful invocation to love which, in its intensity, turns up the erotic heat of the encounter. It seems almost a proclamation of love, not by a messenger as a surrogate but by an ardent lover in person, and Olivia responds in kind with her sudden question about parentage, designed to establish the suitability of this potential husband. Throughout the scene, Viola uses the first person 'I' rather than the third person 'he' as a messenger might use ('he told me to tell you that he loves you', for example): thus the increasingly powerful relationship between them cuts out Orsino almost entirely. Olivia invites Viola to return, but only to hear more of why she cannot love Orsino, and wishes, in her soliloquy, that 'the master were the man' (line 283).

Olivia's quick recognition that she has fallen for Viola/Cesario is likened to a sickness – 'the plague' (line 284) – and this **metaphor** is a brief reminder of the darker side of the play's festive, holiday world (see Themes, on Twelfth Night). She expresses uncertainty about what is happening to her, fearing to find 'Mine eye too great a flatterer for my mind' (line 299) – perhaps she has fallen in love with the looks of this attractive page, rather than made a rational decision about where to bestow her affections. Ultimately, however, she is resigned to see how events unfold, giving – or leaving – control in the hands of fate.

5 **fear no colours** Feste **puns** on 'colours' (military standards) and 'collars' (nooses)

6 **Make that good** explain

8 **good lenten answer** a weak joke

16 **turned away** dismissed

19 **let summer bear it** let the good weather continue, or make it bearable

21 **points** issues, but Maria puns on the sense of laces holding up breeches

23 **gaskins** wide breeches

26 **Eve's flesh** woman

28 **you were best** it would be best for you

32 **Quinapalus** apparently, a made-up 'authority': Feste is mocking scholarly pretensions

36 **Go to** expression of impatience

dry dull, although Feste takes it to mean 'thirsty'

37 **dishonest** unreliable

38 **madonna** Italian for 'my lady', with definite Catholic associations

42 **botcher** cobbler

50 **Misprision** wrongful arrest, and misunderstanding

50–1 **_cucullus ... monachum_** Latin proverb meaning 'the cowl does not make the monk'

52 **motley** the multi-coloured garments traditionally worn by fools and jesters

55 **Dexteriously** dextrously, cleverly

57 **catechize** question, as in religious litany

59 **idleness** recreation, amusement

69 **mend** improve

75 **no fox** not cunning

81 **out of his guard** term from fencing, meaning he has no defence

82 **minister occasion** provide an opportunity

83 **set** fixed, not spontaneous

84 **zanies** professional fools

SCENE 5 continued

87–8 **bird-bolts** blunt arrows for shooting birds

89 **allowed** licensed

92 **Mercury** god of, among other things, deception

98 **well attended** with several attendants

110 ***pia mater*** brain

115–16 **pickle-herring** presumably, these have induced Sir Toby's eponymous belch

116 **sot** fool, drunkard

127 **above heat** above the quantity to warm him

129 **crowner** coroner

    sit hold an inquest

143 **sheriff's post** post set up outside a sheriff or mayor's house, denoting his authority

150 **personage** appearance

152 **squash** unripe peascod

    peascod peapod

153 **codling** unripe apple

153–4 **standing water** at the turn of the tide

154–5 **well-favoured** handsome

155 **shrewishly** like a woman

167 **con** learn by heart

    sustain suffer

168–9 **comptible … usage** I am sensitive to the slightest snub

173 **modest** enough

175 **comedian** actor

185 **forgive** excuse

192 **'Tis not … me** the phases of the moon were associated with lunacy (hence the name)

193 **skipping** inconsequential

196 **swabber** deckhand

    hull anchor

197 **giant** presumably a joking allusion to Maria's height

200 **courtesy** preamble

202 **taxation of homage** demand for payments to a superior noble

203 **matter** meaning, significance

207 **entertainment** reception

211 **text** theme, as for a sermon

213 **comfortable** comforting

223 **curtain** i.e. Olivia's veil

226 **if God did all** if the beauty is natural, not cosmetic

227 **grain** colourfast

228 **blent** blended

229 **cunning** skilful

232 **copy** child, but Olivia takes it to mean 'record'

234 **schedules** lists or inventories

235 **labelled to my will** added to my will

236 **indifferent** quite, fairly

243 **nonpareil** unequalled

244 **fertile** copious

249 **voices well divulged** well spoken of

    free generous, well-bred

251 **gracious** good-looking

257 **willow** associated with unrequited love

258 **my soul** i.e. Olivia

259 **cantons** songs

261 **Hallow** shout, and bless

262 **babbling gossip** personification of the echo

265 **But** unless

267 **state** estate, standing

273 **fee'd post** messenger waiting for a tip

282 **blazon** coat of arms

291 **County** count

293 **flatter with** encourage

300 **owe** own, control

ACT II

SCENE 1   **Antonio and Sebastian, who, it emerges, is Viola's twin brother, discuss their situation. Sebastian is in mourning for his sister and decides to go to Orsino's court; Antonio finds himself in a hostile country where he has many enemies, but will not leave Sebastian because of his love for him**

Antonio has saved Sebastian from the shipwreck in which they believe his twin sister to have been drowned. Sebastian is in cheerless mood, blaming 'the malignancy of my fate' (line 4) for his situation. He seems close to 'unmanly' tears: 'I am yet so near the manners of my mother that ... mine eyes will tell tales of me' (lines 36–7). It appears that the pair do not already know one another well, as Sebastian gives an account of his parentage. Antonio desires to act as his servant, but Sebastian leaves for the court of Orsino. In a **soliloquy** Antonio declares that he will not abandon his friend for 'I do adore thee so / That danger shall seem sport' (lines 42–3).

> The last act ended with Olivia giving up her situation to fate, inviting this mysterious power to 'show thy force' (I.5.300). Sebastian's immediate introduction, therefore, is an direct indication that this power is to be benevolent. In place of the woman Olivia is in love with, a male version, similar in appearance – 'it was said she much resembled me' (lines 22–3) – is introduced. The imagery of fate is immediately echoed by Sebastian – 'My stars shine darkly over me' (line 4), and so even before they meet, the pair are linked by a shared vocabulary to explain events. Similarly, the soon-to-be-lovers are connected by their association with weeping: Sebastian's 'salt-water' remembrance of his dead sister (line 27) links with the 'eye-offending brine' of Olivia's tears for her brother (I.1.31). The gloomy language of Sebastian – 'malignancy', 'evils', 'bad recompense' (lines 3–6) is tempered, however, by our superior knowledge. We know that Viola is not in fact drowned, and our possible suspicion that nor was Sebastian is now confirmed. The parameters of what can, and cannot, happen in the play are thus carefully established, and equally the uncomic spectre of grief which has characterised both twins is registered as mistaken. The firm expectation is of eventual reunion. The scene adds to our knowledge of Viola's situation too: the force of each sibling's feeling of bereavement is strengthened with the information that they are twins, and parallels between Viola and Olivia are further developed with the news that her father, too, has died (line 16).

> The introduction of Antonio in this scene is interesting. His strong feelings for Sebastian, whom he has saved from drowning, are expressed in a structural parallel with the preceding scene,

where Olivia, too, declares her love in a short soliloquy (I.5.298–301). Perhaps the parallel is intended to foreshadow the fact that Olivia and Antonio will, in a sense, be rivals for Sebastian's affections. Lines 42–3 are unexpectedly intense: the word 'adore' denotes a strong familial, perhaps passionate bond. The fact that it is delivered as verse, as opposed to the prose of the rest of the scene, gives it an importance and its speaker a particular status: he is not a 'servant' (line 32) in the sense that, say, Maria is to Olivia. Many productions have made sense of this by casting the relationship between the two men as a homosexual one, or at least suggesting that Antonio has sexual feelings for Sebastian (see Characterisation, and Critical History & Broader Perspectives).

1 **Nor will you not** do you not want me to

3 **darkly** unfavourably

4 **malignancy** bad luck, evil influence (derived from astrology)

5 **distemper** disorder, disturb

9 **determinate** planned

10 **extravagancy** wandering

15 **Messaline** a Shakespearean piece of geography, which may refer to modern-day Marseilles

20 **breach** surf, breaking waves

24 **estimable** appreciative

25 **publish** speak openly of

29 **entertainment** hospitality

31 **murder me** cause me to die (through being parted from you)

35 **kindness** tenderness

36 **manners of my mother** Sebastian means that he is close to weeping (seen as a womanish characteristic)

39 **gentleness** favour

SCENE 2   Malvolio, despatched by Olivia in I.5 to follow Viola with
           a ring, catches up with her. Viola tries to refuse the gift,
           which Malvolio throws down to her before stalking off.
           Viola realises that Olivia has fallen in love with her as
           Cesario, and gives the tangled situation up to time to
           sort out

Malvolio delivers Olivia's message to Orsino's messenger, and presses a
ring upon Viola, who objects that she gave it to Olivia and will not have
it back. Malvolio shows his contempt for her by throwing the ring to the
ground, defying her to pick it up 'if it be worth stooping for' (lines
14–15). After he has gone, Viola muses, in a **soliloquy**, on this strange
turn of events, and concludes 'I am the man!' (line 25). She sees that her
disguise has brought about Olivia's misapprehension, and describes it as
'a wickedness' (line 27) which has the power to shape women's hearts
with a false impression due to 'our frailty' (line 31). She cannot see how
this complicated situation – where she, as a woman, loves her master,
who loves Olivia, who loves her, thinking she is a man – is going to be
resolved, and feels pity for 'poor Olivia' (line 39). Ultimately, it must be
settled by the passage of time: 'O time, thou must untangle this, not I! /
It is too hard a knot for me t'untie' (lines 40–1).

> The prose exchange between Malvolio and Viola confirms
> Malvolio's crabbed character. The scene is, however, most
> significant in giving us Viola's only soliloquy, in which she realises
> that her 'outside' has 'charmed her' (line 19) and that Olivia has
> fallen in love with her. Her immediate reaction is of pity for the
> 'poor lady, she were better love a dream' (line 26), and she
> **apostrophises** her disguise as a form of deceit. Interestingly, Viola's
> response is to make some more general comments about women in
> love, which are worth comparing with Orsino's dismissal of female
> affection as mere 'appetite' (II.4.96) a couple of scenes later. Of
> course, Viola is talking as much about her own plight, helplessly in
> love with Orsino, as she is about Olivia, and thus again draws a
> parallel between their situations. Viola's **rhetorical** questions (lines
> 17, 24, 33 and 36), her interrupted syntax (as at lines 20, 25 and 38)
> and her exclamations (lines 18, 24, 39 and 40) all attest to the
> emotional and psychological disruption caused by this complicated

situation, but perhaps the regularity of the **rhyming couplet** which concludes the scene (lines 40–1) reassures us that all will indeed be well. Perhaps the 'time' to which Viola turns for consolation and resolution will be equal to the time between now and the end of the play.

1 **even** just

4 **but hither** only this far

8 **desperate assurance** certainty that it is hopeless

  she will none of him she will have nothing to do with him

9 **hardy** foolhardy, bold

12 **of** from

15 **in your eye** where you can see it

18 **outside** appearance

  charmed captivated

19 **good view** close examination

20 **lost** made her lose

22 **cunning** craftiness

28 **pregnant enemy** ever watchful enemy (i.e. the devil)

29 **proper false** attractive but deceitful men

30 **set their forms** the image is of women's hearts like molten wax being impressed by men

32 **such as we ... we be** since we are made of frail flesh, we are frail

33 **fadge** turn out

34 **monster** i.e. both man and woman

37 **desperate** hopeless

39 **thriftless** wasted

SCENE 3   Sir Andrew Aguecheek and Sir Toby Belch make merry late in the evening, accompanied by songs from Feste. Maria warns them about the noise they are making, and, indeed, their revelry is interrupted by a furious Malvolio. The revellers take little notice of his threats to tell Olivia of their rowdy behaviour. When he has gone, Toby, Andrew and Maria hatch a plot to humiliate Malvolio by pretending Olivia is in love with him

The two reprobate knights, Sir Andrew and Sir Toby, continue their dedication to indulging their appetites, agreeing that life 'consists of eating and drinking' (line 10–11) (see Themes, on Twelfth Night, and Excess). Feste's contribution is to sing a rather melancholy song about love: 'What's to come is still unsure … Youth's a stuff will not endure' (lines 47–50). Repeating this line as a refrain in Trevor Nunn's film of the play, Ben Kingsley as a mournful Feste quite puts the dampers on Sir Toby and Andrew's inebriated mood. There is an edge of irritation amid the jesting in the exchanges between Sir Andrew and Feste: 'I shall be constrained in't to call thee knave, knight' (lines 65–6). The revelry becomes more and more riotous as Maria warns them that Malvolio is on the warpath, sent by Olivia to 'turn you out of doors' (line 72). Malvolio's entrance sees him turn his contempt on the knights, in a combination of deference and insult: 'My masters, are you mad?' (line 85). He tells them that Olivia is not minded to indulge them in their disorderly conduct even though Sir Toby is her kinsman, and urges him to reform – 'to separate yourself and your misdemeanours' – otherwise 'she is very willing to bid you farewell' (lines 96–8). Malvolio's sobriety – literal and **metaphorical** – is ignored by the revellers, and they challenge his right, as a mere steward, to impose his codes of behaviour on them: 'Dost thou think, because thou art virtuous, there shall be no more cakes and ale?' (lines 111–12).

After Malvolio's exit, Maria tries to calm Sir Toby down, revealing as she does that 'Since the youth of the Count's was today with my lady, she is much out of quiet' (lines 127–9), showing the after-effects of Viola's interview with Olivia. Maria takes on herself the task of repaying Malvolio, promising to 'gull him into a nayword, and make him a common recreation' (lines 130–1). Her plan quickly forms itself: she will 'drop in his way some obscure epistles of love' (lines 148–9), and by faking Olivia's own handwriting, play on Malvolio's own high opinion of himself to make a fool of him. This plan is agreed, and Sir Toby argues it is 'too late to go to bed now' (lines 183–4).

> Here the major subplot, the gulling of Malvolio by the plotters, led by the feisty Maria, is established. The antipathy between Malvolio and the rowdy house-guests might have been anticipated from what we have learnt of each party so far, but here they are brought into open conflict. Malvolio's interruption of the festivities draws up the battle lines: between the hedonistic philosophy of Sir Toby and Sir

Andrew's view of life (lines 9–12) and the 'puritan' austerity of Malvolio's behaviour. While he has a professional responsibility, as steward, to exercise a prudent eye on the household economy, Sir Andrew and Toby are devoted to expense, to drinking and spending. It is a clash between carefulness and extravagance, between restraint and excess, between temperance and immoderation. A late medieval Dutch painting by Pieter Brueghel characterises a similar clash in **allegorical** terms: in 'The Fight between Carnival and Lent' (1559) a figure in the red and yellow motley of the jester leads another in a sombre habit among the revelry of a sixteenth-century festival. No wonder that the audience is usually on the side of the revellers, rather than the party-pooper. There is a wider context for this, too. In suggesting that Malvolio is a 'puritan', Maria evokes a context of religious austerity, as practised by extreme Protestants or, as they were coming to be known, Puritans. One of the chief targets of contemporary Puritan opinion was the theatre. As Stephen Gosson thundered in a pamphlet, 'Plays are the inventions of the devil, the offerings of idolatry, the pomp of wordlings, the blossoms of vanity, the root of apostasy, the food of iniquity, riot and adultery: detest them', and when the Puritans came to power after the Civil War, one of their first acts was to shut all the theatres. Seen in this light, the 'cakes and ale' of Sir Toby's plea might be judged as more than an old drunk's greedy self-indulgence: rather a way of life which includes the theatre itself.

Feste's song in this scene, as in the Epilogue, contributes to the sense of melancholy which is just beneath the play's surface (see Themes, on Twelfth Night), and this is true too of the scene's numerous references to time. Sir Toby classes being up after midnight as a form of early rising – being 'up betimes' (line 2) – whereas Sir Andrew, more prosaically, asserts that 'to be up late is to be up late' (line 5). But in the idea of 'Youth's a stuff will not endure' (line 50), these ungodly hours take on a significance of people trying to beat the clock, live a short life to the full (see Themes, on Twelfth Night). Malvolio. 'a time-pleaser' (line 141), seems to steward hours and minutes as well as drink and money, in contrast to Sir Toby's extravagant spending on all counts. Feste's song, of 'What's to come is still unsure' (line 47), stands as a comment on the action of the play so far in analogy to Olivia's speech at I.5.300–1 and Viola's 'time, thou must untangle this, not I' (II.2.40), and thus serves a **choric** role (see Characterisation).

Maria takes control of the plot of 'revenge' (line 146), despite having been least directly insulted by Malvolio. She has a clear-sighted and merciless view of her victim's weakness, and is described as an Amazon queen, 'Penthesilea' (line 170) in reference to the legendary race of strong women. Perhaps this praise is an early indication of Sir Toby's admiration for her. Malvolio believes that 'all that look on him love him' (line 145) – an echo of Olivia's earlier charge of 'self-love' (I.5.85), and thus the trap is set. Maria's list of her mock-praise of his appearance uses the same **blazon** device – 'the colour of his beard, the shape of his leg, the manner of his gait, the expressure of his eye, forehead and complexion' (lines 149–51) – as Olivia in her praise of Cesario: 'Thy tongue, thy face, thy limbs, actions, and spirit / Do give thee fivefold blazon' (I.5.281–2), thus developing the play's mocking stance towards love conventions and literary clichés (see Themes, on Love & Self-love).

2 **betimes** early

  diluculo surgere part of a Latin proverb, well known from an Elizabethan school textbook. The full proverb '*diluculo surgere saluberrimum est*' means 'to get up at dawn is most healthy'

6 **can** tankard

9 **four elements** i.e. air, earth, fire and water

13 **stoup** tankard holding two pints or one litre

16 **We Three** referring to the caption on popular pictures showing two fools' or asses' heads – the third was the viewer

17 **catch** song sung as a round

18 **breast** lungs for singing

22–3 **Pigrogromitus ... Vapians ... Queubus** probably Sir Toby's imitation of Feste's mock learning

24 **leman** sweetheart

25 **impetticoat** pocket (a nonce word)

  gratility gratuity (again, a nonce word)

27 **Myrmidons** in Greek myth, the race of people led by Achilles. Feste's speech is **bathetic** in stating these obvious absurdities

bottle-ale apparently used to denote inferior ale, hence low-grade taverns

32 **testril** sixpence piece

34 & 36 **good life** the joke is on different meanings: either a drinking song, or a moral song or hymn

40 **sweeting** darling

42 **Every wise man's son** proverbially, wise men were supposed to have foolish sons

52 **contagious** catchy

55 **welkin** sky

56 **souls** music was thought to draw the soul out of the body

58 **dog at** good at

64 **constrained** compelled

73 **Cataian** Chinese – meaning that Olivia is inscrutable

politicians schemers

74 **Peg-a-Ramsey** referring to a ballad about a spying wife, so suggesting that Malvolio is on the lookout

76 **consanguineous** closely related (as Sir Toby goes on to explain)

77 **Tilly-vally** nonsense

79 **Beshrew me** curse me

89 **coziers** cobblers

89–90 **mitigation or remorse of voice** lowering your voices or consideration

92 **Sneck up** roughly equivalent to 'Get lost'

93 **round** blunt

95 **nothing allied** no relation

112 **cakes and ale** traditional festival fare

115–16 **rub your chain with crumbs** a way of cleaning metal; referring to Malvolio's badge of office

119 **uncivil rule** disorderly behaviour

123 **the field** i.e. to a duel

130 **gull** trick

nayword byword (for stupidity)

131 **common recreation** source of general amusement

133 **Possess us** tell us (put us in possession of your thoughts)

141 **time-pleaser** time-server

affectioned affected, pretentious

141–2 **cons state without book** learns elevated language by heart

143 **best persuaded of himself** having a high opinion of himself

150 **expressure** expression

152 **feelingly personated** appropriately described

154 **hands** handwritings

165 **physic** medicine

168 **construction** interpretation

170 **Penthesilea** the Amazonian warrior queen

177 **recover** win

180 **cut** a term of abuse, perhaps referring to a gelding

183 **burn some sack** warm and spice some sack, a white wine from Spain

SCENE 4 Orsino is with his attendants, calling for music, and played for by Feste. Orsino and Viola, disguised as Cesario, discuss love. He argues that women cannot love as strongly as men, and she replies with a story of her 'sister' – really herself – who was so deeply in love and unable to tell of her feelings that she pined away. At the end of the scene, Viola is sent off to Olivia's with another jewel as a love token from Orsino

It is not clear why Olivia's jester, Feste – and we learn that her father too 'took much delight in him' (line 12) – should be playing at Orsino's court, but he is sent for to provide music. Viola's appreciation of the love lyrics of the song leads Orsino to question his servant about whether he/she has known love. Cesario replies with a coded declaration of her love for Orsino, admitting that his/her beloved's appearance and age are about his. Orsino considers this imaginary woman to be too old, telling Cesario that men tire more quickly of love than women: 'Our fancies are more giddy and unfirm, / More longing, wavering, sooner lost and worn, / Than women's are' (lines 33–5).

Feste's song is typically gloomy, this time recounting a lover who dies by the rejection of 'a fair cruel maid' (line 53). In one of his enigmatic speeches, he identifies Orsino's fickleness, calling him 'changeable taffeta' (line 73), and withdraws along with the other attendants to leave Orsino and Viola alone together. Orsino again sends Viola to Olivia, but Viola questions whether his love can ever be returned. She invites Orsino to consider some lady who 'Hath for your love as great a pang of heart / As you have for Olivia' (lines 89–90). Orsino denies that such a love from a woman is possible, asserting that no woman could love as he does. Having just admitted that men are changeable (lines 33–5) he now avows that female bodies cannot 'bide the beating of so strong a passion' (line 93), their hearts 'lack retention' (line 95) and that 'their love may be called appetite' (line 96). Viola tells her own story in disguised form to counter this sexist view: 'My father had a daughter loved a man – / As might be perhaps, were I a woman, / I should your lordship' (lines 106–8). Unable to speak out her love, this woman 'sat like Patience on a monument / Smiling at grief' (lines 113–14). She argues that men make more show of their love, but that women are more constant (lines 115–17). Orsino asks whether this 'sister' died, and this reminds Viola of her drowned brother. She breaks off the conversation to go to Olivia as Orsino had commanded.

> This vital scene (discussed in more detail in Textual Analysis, Text 2) establishes the growth of Viola's feelings for Orsino, and gives her two chances to talk about her love for him, under the disguises of her own love who bears a strong resemblance to him, and the alias of her 'sister' trapped in an unarticulated love. We get an insight into how desperate Viola is to voice her feelings: her disguise has made her utterly alone, since she cannot be herself to anyone. (By contrast, in Shakespeare's earlier play to feature a heroine who dresses as a man, *As You Like It*, Rosalind has her cousin Celia with her who is privy to her disguise, and thus has companionship throughout her masquerade.) The image of the sister pining away for love is an image of fearful anticipation, for Viola is in a situation without obvious (to her) hope of resolution. Perhaps she will never be able to tell Orsino of her love. The sadness underlining the scene is made explicit when the talk of siblings reminds Viola of the loss of her brother. Ultimately, she has to go off again on the unwanted errand of delivering love messages from a man she loves to another woman.

> Another aspect of the scene is how the couple get an unprecedented chance to discuss their ideas about love. Given how regimented conventional aristocratic courtships were in the Elizabethan period,

it would have been highly unlikely that, in her women's clothes, Viola would have been allowed to spend time alone with Orsino if they were not married. One consequence of her disguise is that she is able to gain a kind of intimacy with Orsino in the guise of a man which, **paradoxically**, would be impossible were she to appear as a woman. Trevor Nunn set the scene around various masculine pursuits such as card-playing, smoking, and billiards to symbolise how the Cesario disguise enables Viola to meet and get to know her beloved on male territory.

Orsino's own attitudes seem contradictory. In Act I he praised Olivia for her constancy to the memory of her dead brother, and here he begins by admitting that, indeed, women are more steadfast than men in matters of the heart. He goes on to fulfil Feste's laconic comment on him as 'changeable taffeta' (line 73) by contradicting himself and stating that it is men who are better able to bear the strength of the passion of love, and that women can only offer the brief and quickly sated 'appetite' (line 96) in return (see Textual Analysis, Text 2).

5 **recollected terms** studied phrases (fashionable around the time the play was written)

18 **Unstaid** unsteady

21–2 **very echo ... throned** it reflects the feelings of the heart (thought to be the seat of love)

24 **stayed upon some favour** fixed on some face

30 **wears she to him** adapts herself to him (as clothes to their wearer)

31 **sways she level** exerts a consistent influence

33 **fancies** affections

34 **worn** worn out

35 **think** believe

37 **hold the bent** remain at full stretch (a metaphor from archery)

39 **displayed** opened

44 **spinsters** spinners

45 **free** either 'unattached' or 'carefree'

46 **silly sooth** simple truth

47 **dallies with** lingers on

48 **old age** the good old days, or the golden age of poetry

51 **cypress** either a coffin of cypress wood, or one decked with cypress branches

52 **Fie away** be gone

56 **part** portion

72 **melancholy god** Saturn

73 **changeable taffeta** shot silk, which changes with the light

74 **opal** gemstone which changes with the light

79 **sovereign cruelty** cruel mistress

80 **world** society

82 **parts** status, possessions

83 **giddily** lightly

84 **miracle** Olivia's beauty

85 **pranks** adorns

87 **Sooth** in truth

93 **bide** withstand

95 **retention** the power to retain

97 **motion** impulse

111 **damask** pink and white, like a damask rose

112 **green and yellow** the pallor of melancholy

113 **monument** statue

116 **Our shows ... will** we show more than we feel

123 **denay** denial

SCENE 5   **Sir Toby gains further support against Malvolio, recruiting another member of staff, Fabian, to their cause. Maria leaves the letter for Malvolio to find, and they all hide to watch him take the bait. Malvolio is quickly taken in by Olivia's apparent love letter, and vows to follow its instructions about his dress and demeanour, much to the delighted amusement of the hidden onlookers**

The plot which was hatched in II.3 has quickly taken shape. Fabian is a ready convert to the anti-Malvolio party: he has suffered from Malvolio's antipathy to bear-baiting, a popular spectator sport of the time, opposed by the Puritans and closely allied with the theatre (see Background, on Shakespeare's Theatre). Maria takes charge again, and bustles the conspirators behind the 'box-tree' (line 15) to spy on Malvolio. When

Malvolio enters, he is already musing on Olivia, showing the accuracy of
Maria's jest. Malvolio is convincing himself that some chance remarks by
Olivia and her 'exalted respect' (line 27) for him are a sure sign that she
favours him. Sir Toby is outraged at Malvolio's self-regard: 'Overweening
rogue!' (line 29). Malvolio imagines how he would behave as a Count,
how he would treat his 'kinsman Toby' (line 54), commanding him to
'amend your drunkenness' (line 73), enjoy rich jewels and the
subservience of the household. His vainglorious musings are punctuated
by the unheard exclamations of the onlookers. Picking up the letter left
by Maria, Malvolio quickly perceives that it is in Olivia's writing, and
reads aloud its enigmatic message. Eventually he deduces that the
'M.O.A.I' (line 109) identified in the letter is himself, a conjecture
supported by the mention of the recipient as 'a steward' (line 151). The
letter urges him to 'be opposite with a kinsman, surly with servants' (lines
144–5), to wear 'yellow stockings' and go 'cross-gartered' (lines 148–9),
and to signal his acceptance of the love by smiling in Olivia's presence
(lines 168–9). He promises to do all this. After he has gone, Toby,
Andrew, Fabian and Maria discuss the success of their plot, and look
forward to seeing Malvolio present himself to Olivia following the trick
instructions.

> The plot to punish Malvolio for his strictures against Sir Toby and
> the rest is set in motion, and all goes extremely well. Malvolio's
> 'self-love' (I.5.85) is such that he is already pondering his elevation,
> and how he will use his power as Olivia's husband to lord it over her
> kinsmen. It is not unheard off for social unequals to marry, he
> muses: 'The lady of the Strachy married the yeoman of the
> wardrobe' (lines 38–9), an observation sometimes thought to refer
> to some contemporary piece of court gossip now lost to us.
> Something of his resentment of his lowly situation is revealed in
> this unprompted admission, together with his desire to command
> rather than serve, and to enjoy 'some rich jewel' (line 60) and a
> 'branched velvet gown' (lines 46–7) as well as Olivia herself: 'having
> come from a day-bed, where I have left Olivia sleeping ...' (lines
> 47–8). He is thus ripe for the plot, and Fabian uses the imagery of
> snaring to describe the action: 'now is the woodcock near the gin'
> (line 83). The comedy of these revelations is heightened by the

splenetic interjections of the onlookers, and their unheard commentary on Malvolio's materialistic fantasies.

Malvolio is an object of fun in the scene. Even his account of Olivia's handwriting – 'her very C's, her U's and her T's; and thus makes she her great P's' (lines 86–7) – is a joke at his expense (although one could argue that it is an intentional piece of bawdy revealing the physicality of his desires), punning on the word 'cut' for the female genitalia, and the **homophone** 'P's' = 'pees' = 'urinates'. His puzzling out of '*M.O.A.I*' – scholars have struggled to gloss these letters precisely – reveals the slow-wittedness accompanying his overweening ambition. Sir Toby is so delighted with the success of Maria's plot that he 'could marry this wench' (line 174), and the doltish Sir Andrew's function as his companion's quieter, thinner, echo of agreement is encapsulated in his sequence of risible assents: 'So could I too' (line 175), 'Nor I neither' (line 179), 'Or o'mine either?' (line 182), 'I'll make one too' (line 200) (see Characterisation).

2 **scruple** scrap

3 **boiled to death** Fabian's joke: melancholy was considered a cold humour

5 **sheep-biter** sneaking fellow, or whoremonger

10 **black and blue** thoroughly

12 **An** if

14 **metal of India** gold

17 **behaviour** courtly gestures

19 **contemplative** one who stares vacantly

Close come close, hide

22 **tickling** flattery: trout can be caught in shallow water by stroking them

24 **affect** care for

26 **complexion** temperament

31 **jets** struts

32 **'Slight** God's light – an oath

36 **Pistol** shoot

38–9 **lady of ... wardrobe** a precedent for a woman marrying a social inferior; possibly referring to similar events in at the rival theatre, Blackfriars

40 **Jezebel** unfaithful biblical wife (see 2 Kings 9:30–7)

42 **blows him** puffs him up

44 **state** chair of state

45 **stone-bow** crossbow firing stones

46 **branched** brocaded

51 **humour of state** dignity of rank

52 **demure travel of regard** grave look around

58 **make out** go out

61 **curtsies** bows

63–4 **Though our silence ... peace** something like 'Wild horses wouldn't draw it from me'

66 **familiar** friendly

83 **Now is the woodcock near the gin** now the bird is near the trap

84–5 **the spirit ... to him** Toby is hoping that Malvolio will read the letter aloud

87–8 **her very C's ... P's** 'cut' refers to the female genitalia; P's = urinates

88 **contempt of question** without a doubt

92 **impressure** image of the seal

Lucrece emblem of chastity who committed suicide (hence line 104)

94 **liver** seat of passion

99–100 **numbers altered** meter changed

102 **brock** badger

106 ***sway*** rule

107 **fustian** cheap

111 **dressed** prepared

112 **staniel** kestrel

checks term from hawking, meaning to prepare to pounce

115 **formal capacity** normal intelligence

115–16 **obstruction** obstacle, difficulty

117 **position** arrangement

119 **cold scent** when the hounds have lost the trail of the fox

120 **Sowter** the name of a hound

125 **faults** broken trails

126 **consonancy** consistency

127 **that suffers under probation** that will stand up to scrutiny

135 **simulation** disguise

136 **crush** force

139 ***revolve*** consider

stars fortune and rank

144 ***slough*** a snake's old skin

145 **opposite** hostile

147 **singularity** originality

149 **cross-gartered** a way of fastening the garters around the leg; some critics argue this was a new fashion, some an old, at the time the play was written

154 **champain** open country

155 **open** clear

politic authors writers on political science

156 **baffle** disgrace

157 **point-devise** in every detail

158 **jade** trick

164 **strange** aloof

stout proud

174 **Sophy** ruler or Shah of Persia – probably a reference to Sir Robert Shirley who returned from the Shah in 1599 with a handsome pension, and whose exploits were published

180 **gull-catcher** fool-tricker

183 **play** wager

tray-trip dicing game

189 **aqua-vitae** brandy or other spirit

196 **notable contempt** public disgrace

198 **Tartar** Tartarus, the classical name for hell

ACT III

SCENE 1   Viola and Feste exchange some wordplay as she attempts to gain entrance to Olivia. Viola meets Olivia who declares her love for Cesario. Viola makes her exit saying she cannot reciprocate

Feste's punning begins the scene, and he shows how, as in I.5, 'foolery' can have a serious **satiric** purpose. He equates fools and husbands (lines 31–4), and also makes a comment about Jove sending the clean-cut young Cesario 'a beard' (line 44), a pointed observation sometimes taken to indicate that he knows the truth of the disguise. Feste sums up his role as 'corrupter of words' (lines 34–5); Viola observes that he 'is wise enough to play the fool' (line 58): perhaps Feste knows more about her than he is saying explicitly. Next, Sir Toby and Sir Andrew seem to bar her way to

Olivia. Sir Toby is not friendly, but Olivia and Maria come to meet Orsino's messenger. Sir Andrew listens out for a few choice phrases to help his own woeful attempts to woo Olivia (lines 87–8).

Viola and Olivia's second meeting begins with Viola's attempt to speak on Orsino's behalf, but Olivia will not hear his suit. Olivia reminds her of the ring she sent after her on Viola's last visit (I.5.290–2), and invites Viola to respond: 'What might you think' (line 114). Viola's response is 'pity' and Olivia, desperate for a positive reaction, quickly adds 'That's a degree to love' (line 120). Viola disagrees, and Olivia seems to back away from the intimacy, wishing her messenger well in marriage 'when wit and youth is come to harvest' (line 129). As Viola is about to depart, Olivia recants, pleading, 'Stay' (line 134). They talk at cross-purposes, Viola hinting 'I am not what I am' but unable to reveal herself, Olivia twisting these abstractions to her own purposes (lines 136–40). In the end, Viola tells Olivia that 'no woman' will ever command her heart (line 156), and leaves, with Olivia's final couplet wishing for her return.

> Wordplay, and the gap between words and their meanings, or words and proper communication, are all much in evidence in this scene. Feste argues that a sentence is 'but a cheveril glove to a good wit' (line 12), easily turned inside out, and this twisting of language is characteristic of the misapprehensions in the scene which follows. As a number of characters look set to be made fools of (or make fools of themselves) – Malvolio, Orsino, Olivia, Viola, Sir Andrew – definitions of 'fooling' and 'folly' become rather acute. Feste also makes the link between verbal dexterity and sex: picking up the erotic implications of Viola's word 'dally' (line 14) and applying it to the word 'sister' as a 'wanton' (line 19), and this may be associated with Viola's suggestive description of Olivia's 'most pregnant and vouchsafed ear' (line 86). The scene shows how erotic desire expresses itself in language in the exchange between Olivia and Viola. Small wonder amid these word games that Viola calls herself Olivia's 'fool' (line 141).

> Viola's jesting wordplay with Feste is in prose, but she has a short, philosophical **soliloquy** in verse at lines 58–66, which continues the theme of overlapping wisdom and folly. Meeting Sir Toby and Sir

Andrew, she is more than a match for them, trumping Sir Andrew's French greeting (line 69), with a prompt and fluent reply. Her alert verbal jousting, however, changes abruptly at Olivia's entrance, when she begins to praise her in exalted terms.

When they are alone together, Olivia and Viola's conversation is tense with what is unspoken on both their parts. Olivia's own suppressed feelings break out at line 103 when she interrupts Viola's line, continuing the **pentameter** with her own speech. This happens again at line 107, where it is Viola who makes up Olivia's line, but is interrupted again. By picking up each other's speech rhythms and echoing certain words and phrases, a kind of intimacy is suggested. Viola, it seems, has made two strong attachments – to Orsino and Olivia – while in her disguise. Olivia's following speech gives some indications of her heightened emotional state: lines 114 and 117 are **hypermetric**, and the whole speech is studded with the pronouns 'I' and 'you' in complicated syntax and long sentences. Olivia's diction is fervent: 'shameful cunning' (line 113), 'baited', 'unmuzzled thoughts' (line 116), 'tyrannous' (line 117) – and the burden of this outburst seems to be to blame Cesario for the situation.

The clock interrupts Olivia's concentration (see Themes, on Twelfth Night), but she returns, more urgently than before, to her questioning of Viola. The interchange of single lines (its technical term is **stichomythia**) has a real energy of repressed passion: again, neither woman is able to speak her feelings. There is a kind of desperation in Olivia's 'I would you were as I would have you be' (line 139): having dedicated herself to mourning, she is suddenly overwhelmed by her desires. Orsino warned that she had a great capacity for love if she would only let herself (I.1.34–40): now the force of that stifled emotion has taken hold of Olivia. Both characters speak in end-rhymed verse at the end of the scene, from line 144 onwards. Perhaps this represents a kind of **metaphorical** breathing space from the heightened situation within the confines of rhyme; perhaps it is a way of controlling and curbing a conversation which is getting too hot to handle. That Viola picks up this form too suggests her subliminal responsiveness to Olivia –

perhaps this is one of the subtle aspects of Cesario's conversation which has so attracted her.

Viola can only extricate herself with more half-truths and a kind of verbal trickery worthy of Feste. She comes close to telling Olivia the truth when she states that no woman shall ever 'mistress be [...] save I alone' (line 157), in an instance of doublespeak paralleling her conversation with Orsino about her lover (II.4). This intense scene is the height of the relationship between Olivia and Viola, who never meet again alone (see Textual Analysis, Text 3).

1 **live by** make a living from

2 **tabor** small drum

12 **cheveril** kid leather

14 **dally nicely** play subtly

15 **wanton** (a) equivocal (b) unchaste

20 **bonds disgraced** legal contracts disgraced a man's honesty by implying his word was not to be trusted

33 **pilchers** pilchards

41 **pass upon** jest at

43 **commodity** supply

48 **these** i.e. coins

49 **use** interest

50 **Pandarus** the go-between the lovers in the medieval story of Troilus and Cressida

54 **Cressida was a beggar** in some versions of the story, she was reduced to begging

55 **conster** construe

56 **out of my welkin** not my business

57 **element** sky, or one of the four elements

62 **haggard** hawk
    feather bird

65 **fit** to the point

66 **folly-fallen** fallen into folly

69–70 ***Dieu vous ... serviteur*** (French) God keep you sir! And you too; your servant

72 **encounter** approach, enter

73 **trade** business

75 **list** goal

76 **Taste** try out

81 **prevented** forestalled

86 **pregnant** receptive

vouchsafed attentive

88 **all ready** fully prepared

95 **'Twas never merry world** equivalent to 'Things have never been the same'

96 **lowly feigning** pretence of humility

107 **music from the spheres** ancient astrology held that the heavens made music as they moved

110 **abuse** wrong

112 **construction** interpretation

115–16 **at the stake ... thoughts** the images are from bear-baiting

117 **receiving** perception

118 **cypress** veil of black gauze

121 **grize** flight of steps

vulgar proof common experience

130 **proper** handsome

131 **due west** used **metaphorically** to dismiss Cesario to seek his fortune elsewhere, perhaps with melancholic associations

westward ho! call for passengers by Thames boatmen going to Westminster

145 **love's night is noon** love cannot be hidden

148 **maugre** despite

150–3 **Do not extort ... is better** do not draw the forced conclusion that you should not love me because I have declared my love for you, but rather reflect that love freely given is preferable to love that has been begged

150 **clause** premise

151 **For that** because

SCENE 2   **Sir Toby eggs Sir Andrew on to challenge his rival Cesario to a duel. We hear that Malvolio is wearing cross garters and yellow stockings**

Sir Andrew feels aggrieved that Olivia has done 'more favours on the Count's serving-man than ever she bestowed upon me' (lines 4–5). Fabian argues that this was a ploy to make Andrew jealous, but that he has missed his opportunity to capitalise on this. He is in danger of losing her favour, 'unless you do redeem it by some laudable attempt either of valour or policy' (lines 26–8). Sir Toby suggests that a duel is the perfect solution, and despatches Andrew to write out the challenge. Fabian remarks that Andrew is 'dear' (line 51), but Sir Toby's response takes this as a measure of monetary rather than personal value, suggesting he endures his friendship because of the money: 'I have been dear to him, lad, some two thousand strong or so' (lines 52–3). Fabian and Sir Toby guess that the forthcoming duel will be evenly matched between the bloodless Sir Andrew and his soft-looking and youthful opponent. Maria enters to tell them that Malvolio has enacted all the commands in their counterfeit letter, and promises a rare sight: 'if you desire the spleen, and will laugh yourselves into stitches, follow me' (lines 64–5): her entrance at this point and her account of the extraordinary figure of the transformed Malvolio is to whet our eagerness to see this comical sight for ourselves – but not yet.

Orsino in I.1, Antonio in II.1, Viola in II.4, Malvolio in II.5, Olivia in III.1, and now Andrew Aguecheek joins the ranks of the play's largest cast – those who are unlucky or unhappy or unrequited in love. Fabian and Sir Toby encourage him to the duel, despite having apparently little regard for his martial qualities: 'awake your dormouse valour' (line 18). There is a hint that Sir Toby's greed is his motive for the friendship with Sir Andrew, perhaps anticipating his explicit cruelty in V.1.203–4. But many critics and theatre directors have felt that the play's rhythm falters with this long but rather slight scene and have found difficulty in keeping up the pace established by the action so far.

10 **argument** proof

12 **'Slight** by God's light!

15 **grand-jury men** these jurors decided whether there was sufficient evidence for a case to go to a full trial

18 **dormouse** sleeping, or timid

23 **baulked** shirked

    double gilt twice-gilded (of gold), therefore, twice as lucky

25 **north of my lady's opinion** disfavour, coldness

26 **Dutchman's beard** this may be a contemporary allusion to William Barentz who led an expedition to the Arctic in 1596–7

28 **policy** political strategy

30 **Brownist** member of an extreme Puritan group founded by Robert Browne and advocating the separation of church and state

31 **me** i.e. on my advice

40–1 **curst and brief** sharp and to the point

42 **licence of ink** the freedom given by writing rather than speaking

43 **'thou'-est** call him 'thou' – as a social inferior

45 **bed of Ware** a famous Elizabethan bed, now in the V&A museum in London, measuring eleven feet square

46 **gall** (a) bitterness (b) ingredient of ink

50 **cubiculo** Toby's affected Italian word for 'bedroom'

51 **manikin** puppet

57 **wain-ropes** wagon-ropes pulled by oxen

58 **hale** haul, drag

60 **anatomy** corpse

63 **youngest wren** the youngest wren was usually the smallest of the brood

64 **the spleen** a fit of laughter, thought to come from the spleen

66 **renegado** renegade, literally, a Christian converted to Islam

68 **impossible passages of grossness** wildly unlikely statements

71 **pedant** schoolmaster

75–6 **the new map ... Indies** a new map by Emmeric Mollineux published in 1599 drew the East Indies more fully than previously

SCENE 3   Antonio has followed Sebastian, who is pleased to see him. Antonio is in danger in Illyria, so he retires to an inn, leaving his purse with Sebastian for his convenience

At the end of II.1, Sebastian left Antonio for Orsino's court. Here, Antonio catches up with him, explaining that his 'desire, / More sharp than filèd steel, did spur me forth' (lines 5–6). His concern for Sebastian as a stranger in a land which might be 'rough and inhospitable' (line 11) has prompted his actions. Sebastian is grateful for his care. Antonio tells him that he is unable to 'go see the reliques of this town' (line 19) since, after a seafight in which some of Orsino's men were killed and goods seized, he is at risk of arrest. He goes to the English-sounding inn the Elephant, leaving Sebastian with his money in case he sees 'some toy / You have desire to purchase' (lines 45–6).

The purpose of this scene seems to be to remind us about Sebastian, and to stress the bond with Antonio. The information about Antonio's past dealings with the Illyrians shows that he has put himself in great danger by following Sebastian: he is about the only character in the play who, it could be argued, acts selflessly in the service of someone he loves (see Characterisation). Sebastian, by contrast, seems rid of the burden of grief which characterised his previous appearance. His speeches are brief – perhaps indicative of embarrassment: the repetition of 'thanks' (lines 15 and 16) may suggest he does not know how to respond appropriately, or that he cannot find a way to thank Antonio for his care. He is quickly, however, on to lighter topics, keen to go sightseeing, unperturbed by Antonio's revelations and perhaps immaturely fascinated at an older man's tales of adventure on the seas: 'Belike you slew a great number of his people?' (line 30).

The nature of Antonio's past crimes is not made clear, and there is some discrepancy between his dismissal of Sebastian's curiosity about killings – 'Th'offence is not of such a bloody nature' (line 31) – and the later account of events in V.1.

6 **not all** not only

8 **jealousy** concern

9 **skill-less in** unacquainted with

12 **rather** more quickly

15 **ever oft** very often

16 **uncurrent** not legal tender

17 **worth** wealth

   conscience sense of indebtedness

19 **reliques** sights, antiquaries

24 **renown** make famous

26 **Count his** count's

29 **ta'en** captured

   scarce be answered difficult to make reparation

30 **Belike** perhaps

32 **quality** circumstances

33 **bloody argument** reason for bloodshed

35 **traffic's** trade's

37 **lapsèd** apprehended

40 **Elephant** name of an inn near the Globe theatre in Southwark

41 **bespeak our diet** order our food

45 **Haply** perhaps

     toy trifle, knick-knack

46 **your store** your money

47 **idle markets** unnecessary expenditure

SCENE 4   Olivia is greeted by the grotesque sight of a smiling,
yellow-stockinged, cross-gartered Malvolio. Sir Toby
promises to calm him down in a darkened room. Sir
Andrew's challenge to Cesario is read out. Viola returns at
Olivia's command. Sir Toby delivers the challenge and
describes Sir Andrew's ferocity. Sir Toby encourages Sir
Andrew to fight Viola; Antonio enters and thinks it is
Sebastian who is in danger. Before he can do anything he
is arrested, and he appeals to 'Sebastian' for help, but
Viola replies that she does not know him. After he has
been taken away, Viola wonders whether the mystery
might mean that Sebastian is still alive

Olivia is preoccupied by thoughts of Cesario, but these are pushed away
by Malvolio's extraordinary entrance, heralded by Maria. She warns that
he 'is sure possessed', because 'he does nothing but smile' (lines 9–11).
Olivia identifies a similarity between them, for she, too, is mad – for love.
When Malvolio enters, his greeting 'Sweet lady' (line 17) marks his jovial
and intimate manner. His uncharacteristic chatter leads Olivia to suggest
he goes to bed to recover; he takes this as a sexual invitation and promises
'I'll come to thee' (lines 29–30). Quoting phrases from the letter she
purportedly wrote him, he is greeted with growing incredulity and
concern by Olivia who, of course, does not recognise their significance.
She concludes that this catalogue of bizarre comments are 'very
midsummer madness' (line 56) (see Themes, on Madness). Into this
scene comes news of Cesario's return. Olivia despatches Malvolio to be
looked after by her kinsman Sir Toby, but Malvolio takes this for an
excuse to see him perform the other part of her supposed instructions to
him: to be rude with Sir Toby. When the knight enters, Malvolio behaves

as he has been commanded by the letter, culminating in the curse 'Go, hang yourselves all' (line 122).When he has gone, the conspirators decide to continue the jest and develop Olivia's diagnosis of madness in her steward: they will imprison him in a 'dark room' 'for our pleasure and his penance' (lines 134–6).

At Sir Andrew's entrance the scene turns to another letter: the challenge to Cesario. Maria tells him his chance is at hand, as Cesario is about to arrive, and Sir Toby eggs his friend on to 'draw, and as thou drawest, swear horrible' (lines 175–6). After he has gone, Sir Toby reveals that he will not deliver the pusillanimous letter, which would cut no ice with Cesario; 'he will find it comes from a clodpole' (line 186). Instead he will convey a fear-inducing report of Sir Andrew to Cesario. When Viola enters, Olivia is initially apologetic: 'I have said too much unto a heart of stone' (line 197), and Viola repeats that she wants only her love for Orsino. She agrees to return again the following day. Sir Toby and Fabian waylay Cesario to tell of the challenge from Sir Andrew, 'full of despite, bloody as the hunter, [who] attends thee at the orchard end' (lines 218–20). Viola responds to their descriptions of this violent assailant with apologies, admitting 'I am no fighter' (line 247) and agrees with their proposal to try and placate the bellicose knight. Meanwhile, Sir Toby tells Sir Andrew that Cesario 'has been fencer to the Sophy' (line 272) and cannot be pacified. Thus the two unwilling parties are brought to the brink of fighting by Sir Toby's provocations.

Antonio enters to see someone he believes to be his beloved Sebastian under threat from an armed knight. He immediately intervenes to take Sebastian's quarrel on himself, but the officers enter to arrest him 'at the suit / Of Count Orsino' (lines 318–19). Under arrest, Antonio requests the return of the purse he gave Sebastian, but this is not Sebastian, and so his request is answered with bewilderment: 'What money, sir?' (line 331). Antonio cannot believe that he should be denied when in such need of his friendship, particularly when Viola tells him how much she hates 'ingratitude' (line 345). Antonio tells the assembled officers that he saved 'This youth that you see here … out of the jaws of death' (lines 350–1), and upbraids 'Sebastian' for his unkindness. Viola's **aside** shows that she can hardly dare believe 'That I, dear brother, be now ta'en for you' (line 367). Viola admits that she and Sebastian look alike, especially in her disguise: 'I my brother know / Yet living in my glass. Even such and so / In favour was my brother; and he went / Still in this fashion, colour, ornament, / For him I imitate' (lines 370–4).

A number of plots come together in this long scene. Maria's scheme against Malvolio comes to fruition as the steward makes a fool of himself in front of Olivia. The parallel plots of the twins connect in Antonio's mistaking of Viola for Sebastian, and the hope this gives her that Sebastian is not drowned takes the plot a good step towards resolution. Getting all these intrigues working together takes a good deal of stage-management, and Shakespeare is aware that this is all rather unlikely. As Fabian wryly notes, 'If this were played upon a stage now, I could condemn it as an improbable fiction' (lines 126–7). By pre-empting our disbelief, the play makes it almost impossible to remain aloof from its machinations.

Malvolio's humiliation is not subtle, but is often extremely funny when played in the theatre. The contrast between the uptight 'Puritan' of the earlier scenes and the grinning, lascivious fashion victim of this scene is pointed (see Characterisation), and Olivia's view that he is mad gives the plotters an idea of how to continue the torture of their victim. Olivia herself identifies that Malvolio's apparent madness is an acute example of the way in which a number of the characters make fools of themselves: 'I am as mad as he / If sad and merry madness equal be' (lines 14–15), thinking, no doubt, of the protestations of love she pressed on an unwilling Cesario at their last meeting and for which she makes a kind of apology on his return. After the passionate exchanges of III.1, this meeting is rather formal, even stilted – a short verse interlude amid a scene of lively prose. They do not meet again until the last scene. A more immediate assault to Viola's masculine disguise is in the manufactured threat from Sir Andrew, as exacerbated by Sir Toby. Viola is keen to try to pacify her opponent, as is he, but both are manipulated into fighting by Sir Toby, presumably for his own amusement at watching. Her aside 'a little thing would make me tell them how much I lack of a man' (lines 293–4) is a shared joke with the audience, with a bawdy **pun** of precisely what 'little thing' of a man's it is she lacks (see Themes, on Gender).

Antonio's intervention in the scene brings with it a note of potential tragedy. His verse denunciations of the apparent ingratitude of his friend Sebastian are based on a misunderstanding, but they do foreshadow the way in which his kindnesses to the man he saved from the shipwreck will be increasingly eclipsed by other, more pressing relationships in the rest of the play. He rails, in a slightly disconnected vein, on the 'beauteous evil' of Sebastian's outward appearance, which promises good but hides an inner blemish (lines 356–61): the language of idolatry – 'idol', 'god' – express the strength, perhaps the excessive strength, of his emotions (see Themes, on Excess, and Love & Self-love). Interestingly, his portrayal of a man he believes to be Sebastian stresses a disparity between external and internal appearance, and is thus an appropriate description of the disguised Viola herself. The speech is a darker version of Viola's own 'disguise, I see thou art a wickedness' (II.1.27). It is only when Viola is mistaken for her brother that she reveals explicitly that she has fashioned her disguise on his appearance, thus retrospectively providing a reason for her adoption of male clothes in the first place: as a symptom of grief and a way of keeping the supposedly dead sibling 'alive'. That her twin brother might not be dead after all is a sudden and welcome possibility: this scene begins to untangle the 'knot' (II.2.41) of the plot's complications.

1 **he says** supposing he says

2 **bestow of** give

5 **sad and civil** grave and respectful

9 **possessed** mad, possessed by devils

22 **sonnet** song

    'Please one and please all' the refrain of a popular bawdy ballad of the time

25 **black in my mind** humoral theory held that melancholy was caused by excess black bile

26 **It** i.e. Maria's letter

27 **Roman hand** newly fashionable italic handwriting

29–30 **Ay ... thee** another quotation from a bawdy ballad

35 **daws** jackdaws

56 **midsummer madness** proverbial remark, indicating the height of madness

63 **miscarry** come to harm

65 **come near me** begin to understand who I am

74 **sir of note** renowned person

75 **limed** snared

80 **incredulous** incredible

85 **drawn in little** contracted to a small size

Legion used of the devils possessing the madman in Mark 5:9.

89–90 **private** privacy

102 **water** urine

wisewoman herbalist

109 **move** upset

111 **rough** violent

112 **bawcock** fine bird

115 **biddy** shortened form of chickabiddy, hen

116 **gravity** a man of dignity

cherry-pit children's game of throwing cherry stones into a hole

117 **foul collier** dirty coalman, an allusion to the devil's blackness

123 **element** sphere

128 **genius** soul

130–1 **take air, and taint** be spoilt through exposure (it was believed that fresh air was bad for fevers)

134–5 **dark room and bound** the usual treatment for madness

139 **to the bar** into the open

139–40 **a finder of madmen** one of the jury judging whether the defendant was mad

141 **matter for a May morning** holiday sport

144 **saucy** (a) impudent (b) spicy

149 **admire** marvel

154 **in thy throat** deeply

163 **windy side** safe side

167–8 **as thou usest him** as much as you treat me like one

171 **commerce** conversation

173 **Scout me for him** look out for him for me

174 **bum-baily** contemptuous term for a bailiff (because they crept up on debtors from behind)

178 **approbation** credit

proof trial

186 **clodpole** blockhead

192 **cockatrices** mythical monsters able to kill with a look

193 **Give them way** keep out of their way

194 **presently** immediately

198 **unchary** unguardedly

202 **'haviour** manner

204 **jewel** jewelled miniature painting

208 **honour ... give** that can be granted without compromising my honour (i.e. virginity)

211 **acquit you** set you free

218 **despite** defiance

219–20 **Dismount thy tuck** draw thy sword

220 **yare** prompt

227 **opposite** opponent

230 **unhatched** never drawn

231 **carpet consideration** courtly rather than military reasons

233 **incensement** anger

235 **Hob, nob!** come what may

237 **conduct** escort

239 **taste** test

241 **computent** to be reckoned with

245 **meddle** duel

248 **know of** inquire of

255 **mortal arbitrement** trial by combat to the death

259 **form** outward appearance

268 **firago** virago, fighting woman

    pass duelling bout

269 **stuck-in** thrust

269 **mortal** deadly

270 **answer** return blow

271 **pays** kills, finishes

272 **Sophy** Shah of Persia

280 **motion** proposal

281 **perdition of souls** killing

298 *duello* code of duelling

309 **undertaker** one who undertakes a duel on another's behalf

316 **reins well** is easily controlled

320 **favour** face

328 **amazed** bewildered

329 **be of comfort** cheer up

336 **my present** what I have at present

337 **coffer** money

339 **deserts** services deserving of reward

340 **persuasion** the power to persuade

352 **sanctity** love as for a sacred object

354 **venerable** worthy of veneration

356 **vild** vile

359 **unkind** hard-hearted

361 **o'er-flourished** richly decorated

369 **saws** sayings

371 **glass** mirror

374 **prove** prove true

376 **dishonest** dishonourable

380 **religious** committed

385 **event** result

386 **yet** after all

ACT IV

SCENE 1   Feste greets Sebastian as Cesario, bidding him return to
Olivia. Sir Andrew also mistakes Sebastian for his twin,
and in the ensuing fight, is bettered by his adversary.
Olivia enters and takes a surprised but apparently willing
Sebastian away to her house

When Sebastian denies that he is the object of Feste's errand, his
language is the topsy-turvy idiom of fooling: 'thou art a foolish fellow'
(line 3). Feste responds with a knowing series of negatives, concluding
'Nothing that is so, is so' (line 8), an apt summary of the reigning
confusions of the plot. Feste's mistake is repeated by Sir Andrew and Sir
Toby, who believe that Sebastian is Cesario, and resume the quarrelling
terms of the previous scene. Sebastian does not hesitate to defend
himself, such that Sir Andrew vows 'I'll have an action of battery against
him, if there be any law in Illyria' (lines 33–4). Sir Toby and Sebastian are
squaring up to each other when Olivia enters, seeing, with dismay, her
kinsman and her beloved 'Cesario' about to fight. For the first time in the

play, she chastises Sir Toby for his behaviour: 'ungracious wretch' (line 46) and 'Rudesby' (line 50), soothing 'Cesario' and inviting him 'Go with me to my house' (line 53). Sebastian's **aside** suggests that he cannot believe her attentions towards him, but that he is enjoying them is clear: 'If it be thus to dream, still let me sleep!' (line 62). He and Olivia exit together.

This scene introduces Olivia to the male twin who will resolve her passionate attraction to Cesario, and, although the exchange between her and Sebastian is brief, we are given to understand that Sebastian is quite happy with the attentions of this unknown woman. Feste's misunderstanding serves to bring the pair together, and, incidentally, to prompt Olivia to some harsh words to her layabout uncle Sir Toby. The words 'fool', 'folly', and 'foolish' which are bandied around between Sebastian and Feste highlight the absurdity of a disordered situation which is coming to a resolution.

5 **held out** kept up

9 **vent** utter

13 **lubber** lout

14 **cockney** one using affected language

ungird thy strangeness drop your formality

17 **foolish Greek** buffoon

21 **report** reputation

22 **fourteen years' purchase** since Elizabethan land prices were usually twelve times the annual rent, this means a large sum

38 **fleshed** blooded, initiated into combat

43 **malapert** impudent

50 **Rudesby** ruffian

52 **extent** assault

55 **botched up** patched together

57 **Beshrew** curse

58 **started** roused (a term from hunting)

59 **What relish is in this?** What does this mean?

60 **Or ... or** either ... or

61 **Lethe** mythical river inducing oblivion

63 **Would thoud'st** if only you would

SCENE 2   Dressed as Sir Topas the priest, Feste taunts the
           imprisoned Malvolio and tries to make him believe
           he is mad

The plot against Malvolio takes on a darker aspect with the new involvement of Feste, not previously part of the scheming. Malvolio believes that Sir Topas will bring him relief, begging 'do not think I am mad' (line 29), but Sir Topas is set on making Malvolio believe he has lost his wits. He argues that the house is not in fact dark, but it is Malvolio's madness that makes it appear so to him. Before an audience of Maria and Sir Toby, he encourages him in disquisitions on matters pseudo-philosophical – Pythagoras's opinion 'concerning wildfowl' (lines 49–50), then returns in his own guise to continue to torment Malvolio. The steward requests pen and paper to write to Olivia about his treatment; singing and jesting, Feste promises to return.

> The treatment of Malvolio in this scene brings out the latent cruelty inherent in comedy, and offers a darker perspective on Feste's role (see Characterisation). The play's insistent questioning of categories of madness and sanity, or wisdom and folly (see Themes, on Madness) is also brought to the fore. 'I am as well in my wits, fool, as thou art', says a frightened Malvolio. 'Then you are mad indeed, if you be no better in your wits than a fool', is Feste's unpitying retort (lines 88–90). Feste's disguise as Sir Topas is also significant as a malicious version of the deceits practised elsewhere in the play.

2 **Topas** the topaz stone had the medical property of curing lunacy

8 **said** called

  a good housekeeper hospitable

9 **careful** conscientious

10 **competitors** partners-in-crime

12 **Bonos dies** good day, in mock Latin

12–13 **hermit of Prague** this seems to be a bogus scholarly authority invented by Feste

14 **Gorboduc** king of ancient Britain, subject of the earliest English tragedy (1561)

25 **hyperbolical** raging

33 **house** a room

36–7 **barricadoes** barricades

37 **clerestories** high windows

44 **Egyptians in their fog** a plague of darkness was visited on the Egyptians in Exodus 10:21–3

47 **abused** wronged

48 **constant question** logical discussion

49 **Pythagoras** ancient Greek philosopher who held that the soul could inhabit different bodies in succession (the theory of transmigration)

62 **I am for all waters** I can turn my hand to anything

74 **perdy** by God (corruption of par Dieu)

86 **five wits** the five faculties were wit, imagination, fantasy, estimation and memory

91 **propertied me** treated me like a piece of furniture

93 **face** bully

94 **Advise you** be careful

100 **God buy you** God be with you

104 **shent** scolded

109 **Well-a-day** Alas

123 **old Vice** predecessor of the Elizabethan stage fool in earlier morality dramas

127 **'Pare thy nails** apparently a familiar piece of stage business for the Vice

     dad some plays cast the Vice as the son of the devil

SCENE 3   Sebastian wonders at the turn of events. Olivia brings a priest to Sebastian to solemnise their rapid union

Sebastian's **soliloquy** reviews Olivia's treatment of him and it seems he can hardly believe his luck: ''tis wonder that enwraps me thus', 'not madness' (lines 3–4). He also muses on Antonio's disappearance, expressing a need for 'counsel' since his 'soul disputes well with my sense' (line 9). Sebastian realises that there is something going on that he does not understand, but any misgivings are swept away by Olivia's entrance with the priest. She tells Sebastian that they must marry immediately so that 'my jealous and too doubtful soul / May live at peace' (lines 27–8), although their union can be kept a secret. Sebastian agrees, and they go off with the priest for the ceremony.

Sebastian's rapid assent to a proposal of marriage from a woman he has hardly met may seem surprising (see Characterisation). The poet W.H. Auden felt this sudden and unprompted acceptance reflected badly on him, but, to be fair, Sebastian's soliloquy does show him bewildered by events. Like many other characters in the play he wonders if he is mad, repeated at lines 4, 10 and 15, or whether it is 'the lady' (he never calls her by her name: presumably he does not know it) who is 'mad' (line 16). On this last point, Sebastian rationalises that she could not manage her household were she insane (see Themes, on Madness). His wish for Antonio's advice shows how much he, like Viola, is alone in this extraordinary situation. Obviously the substitution of Sebastian for 'Cesario' in Olivia's hastily arranged marriage has a clockwork neatness, perhaps exemplified in the two **rhyming couplets** which conclude the scene (lines 32–5).

6 **was** had been

11 **accident** unexpected event

12 **discourse** reasoning

17 **sway** rule

18 **dispatch** orders

21 **deceivable** deceptive

24 **chantry by** nearby chapel (a chantry was where masses for the souls of the dead were said)

26 **Plight me the full assurance** a betrothal in front of a priest was as legally binding as a full marriage service

29 **Whiles** until

31 **birth** nobility

ACT V

SCENE 1   **The denouement! Antonio is arrested and tells them about Sebastian. Cesario is greeted warmly by Olivia, and denounced by Orsino when he hears of their marriage. Sebastian's entry resolves the situation. Orsino resolves to marry Viola. Viola and Sebastian are reunited. The plot against Malvolio is revealed and he swears revenge**

At Olivia's house, Fabian and Feste are discussing the letter Feste agreed to deliver for the imprisoned Malvolio at the end of IV.2. Orsino and

Viola arrive, and Orsino engages in some banter with Feste over money. Antonio is brought in by the officers, and Orsino recognises him from his brave and skilful fighting, when even his enemies 'Cried fame and honour on him' (line 57). The officer tells Orsino that Antonio was involved in a skirmish in which 'your young nephew Titus lost his leg' (line 60), but Viola comments that he did her kindness. Orsino hails Antonio as 'pirate' (line 66), but Antonio denies this charge: he was never 'thief or pirate', but only 'Orsino's enemy' (lines 72–4). He continues to mistake Viola – 'that most ingrateful boy there by your side' (line 75) – for her brother, rehearsing the debts Sebastian owes him for his life. He reveals that he has spent three months with Sebastian before arriving in Illyria that day; Orsino confidently asserts that Viola has spent the previous three months with him. Olivia's entrance sees further confusion. She thinks she sees the Cesario she has married, and upbraids him: 'you do not keep promise with me' (line 101). Orsino professes his continued love for Olivia, but realises that Olivia is in love with Cesario. His rage culminates in his threat to Viola: 'I'll sacrifice the lamb that I do love' (line 128). She replies that she loves Orsino more 'than e'er I shall love wife' (line 134). When Olivia pronounces herself 'beguiled', Viola is perplexed: 'Who does beguile you?' (lines 137–8). When Olivia calls her 'husband' (line 141), both Viola and Orsino are astonished. Olivia sends for the priest to confirm her story, and he corroborates her claim: he married the pair 'but two hours' ago (line 161). Orsino declares that he and Cesario will never again meet, but the moment is interrupted by Sir Andrew, who calls for a doctor to tend his broken head, injured by Cesario. Viola denies that she has done him any hurt. Sir Toby enters, also wounded, and refuses Sir Andrew's offers of help: 'Will you help? An asshead, and a coxcomb, and a knave – a thin-faced knave, a gull' (lines 203–4).

As Sir Toby, Sir Andrew, Feste and Fabian leave, Sebastian enters, apologising to Olivia for having hurt her relative. He begs her pardon, noting that she looks strangely at him, 'and by that / I do perceive it hath offended you' (lines 209–10). Orsino realises that there are two: 'one face, one voice, one habit, and two persons!' (line 213). Sebastian sees Antonio, who wonders which of the pair is Sebastian. When Sebastian comes face to face with Viola, he wonders 'Do I stand there?' (line 222). Through mutual questioning about their father, the twins come to recognise each other, and Viola promises to get her 'maiden weeds' (line 252) back from the sea captain to prove it. Sebastian turns to Olivia to observe that she is 'betrothed both to a maid and a man' (line 260), but before she can reply, Orsino is taking stock of the revelations, recalling how Cesario vowed never to love woman as she loved Orsino, and taking her hand.

Viola reports that the captain is being held by Malvolio, which reminds Olivia of her benighted steward. Feste enters with Malvolio's letter, and this is read aloud. In it, Malvolio claims that Olivia wrongs him in her treatment since he has her letter instructing him in the behaviours for which he has been imprisoned. Olivia calls for him to be brought to her. In the meantime, Olivia names herself sister to Orsino and to Viola, and Orsino instructs his page: 'you shall from this time be / Your master's mistress' (line 323). Malvolio gives Olivia the counterfeit letter, which she identifies as being like her handwriting, but written by Maria. She promises to get to the bottom of the mystery, but Fabian confesses that he, Maria and Sir Toby manufactured the trick, and that Sir Toby has married Maria in 'recompense' (line 362) for her part in it. He urges it be taken as a joke which 'may rather pluck on laughter than revenge' (line 364) if both sides of the argument are taken into account. Feste gloats in his revenge; as he storms out, Malvolio swears 'I'll be revenged on the whole pack of you' (line 375). Orsino ends the scene, addressing Cesario whose women's clothes have not yet been returned, although promising that when they do, she shall be 'Orsino's mistress and his fancy's queen!' (line 385).

Alone on stage, Feste sings a melancholic song with the refrain, 'For the rain it raineth every day'. His final lines bring the performance to a close: 'But that's all one, our play is done, / And the rain it raineth every day' (lines 404–5).

> This finale is a dazzlingly orchestrated resolution of the different strands of the plot, as almost all the players are brought together on stage and to revealing their loves. The highly charged emotions of these serial revelations are expressed in frequent references to madness (carried over from Malvolio's scene in the darkened room in Act IV) and to witchcraft (for example at line 74). As the play moves towards resolution, however, there are final convolutions: Olivia believes her new husband disdains her when Viola expresses

her love, Orsino threatens to kill Cesario for his duplicity in marrying Olivia, and Malvolio promises revenge on the 'whole pack' (line 375). Only this last twist remains unresolved at the end of the play.

The flurry of declarations and revelations means that the long scene is structured around short and concentrated exchanges between the various true and false pairings, between Olivia and Orsino, Olivia and Viola, Viola and Sebastian, Viola and Orsino, Sebastian and Antonio, with interruptions from Sir Toby, Sir Andrew, Feste and Malvolio. The spotlight of emotional intensity pinpoints different moments and combinations as all are brought to reveal their most passionate feelings of love. Orsino's love is close to hate, and is articulated primarily as a threat – 'Him I will tear out of this cruel eye' (line 125) – and in this he is close to the violence expressed by Malvolio and which comes from Antonio's description of his skirmishes with Orsino's forces.

The play may seem to work towards a happy ending, in which not only lovers are restored but a brother is returned to Viola and Olivia gains Orsino as a brother. There are, however, those left out in the **metaphorical** cold. Sir Andrew has nothing to show for his expensive sojourn in Olivia's household; Antonio is soon forgotten when Sebastian is reunited with Viola; Feste is still singing his own mournful songs. Even the lovers may be thought to have been over-hastily paired off: with Orsino's sudden proposal to his quondam page and Olivia's silent acceptance of her mystery husband suggesting an ending that owes more to dramatic convention than to emotional veracity. Michael Pennington notes that the final marriages 'have something perfunctory about them as if the fantastic contortions of the plot had made the characters into puppets'. We never see Viola back in her own clothes, although there are many references to them (see Themes, on Gender), and thus the homoerotic tinge of the relationship between Orsino and Cesario is daringly preserved, nor does she allow her brother to embrace her (line 248). The bitter-sweet mood of the play is encapsulated in the final scene's careful balance of feeling and choreography: *Twelfth Night,* as befits a play about the end of the festive season, has a melancholic edge to its final celebrations (see Themes, on Twelfth Night).

20–1 **four negatives make your two affirmatives** the jest suggests that no, no, no, no can be recalculated as yes, yes on the principle of the double negative becoming a positive

34 ***Primo, secundo, tertio*** Latin for first, second, third

35 **the third pays for all** third time lucky

50 **Vulcan** in Roman mythology, smith to the gods

51 **baubling** trivial

52 **unprizable** worthless

53 **scatheful** destructive

54 **bottom** ship

58 **fraught** cargo

   Candy Candia, now Crete

61 **desperate of** disregarding

   state danger

62 **brabble** brawl

64 **put strange speech upon me** spoke to me in a strange manner

68 **dear** dire

77 **wrack** person who has been shipwrecked

79 **retention** reservation

81 **pure** purely

86 **face me out** deny to my face

87 **removèd thing** stranger

89 **recommended** committed

107 **fat and fulsome** gross, nauseating

111 **ingrate** ungrateful

116 **th'Egyptian thief** alluding to a popular story in which a brigand tried to kill his captive to prevent her being captured by his enemies

119 **non-regardance** oblivion

121 **screws** wrenches

123 **minion** sexual favourite (disparaging term)

126 **his master's spite** to spite his master

134 **More by all mores** beyond comparison

137 **detested** denounced

145 **strangle thy propriety** deny your identity (as my husband)

SCENE 1 continued

163 **grizzle** grey hairs

    case fox skin

164 **craft** craftiness

174 **coxcomb** head

178 **incardinate** Sir Andrew's mistake for 'incarnate' – in human form

188 **set nothing** think nothing of

189 **halting** limping

191 **othergates** otherwise

196 **set** closed

197 **passy-measures pavin** a stately dance

201–2 **be dressed** have our wounds dressed

203 **coxcomb** fool

207 **the brother of my blood** my own brother

208 **with wit and safety** with sensible self-protection

214 **perspective** optical illusion

218 **Fear'st** do you doubt

224 **deity** godlike power

226 **blind** indifferent

231 **So went he suited** he was dressed in this way

232 **spirits** devils

    form and suit body and appearance

234 **dimension** physical form

    grossly naturally

235 **participate** have in common with others

236 **as the rest goes even** as everything else fits

246 **lets** hinders

249 **cohere** coincide

    jump agree

252 **weeds** clothes

257 **to her bias drew** followed her inclination

263 **wrack** shipwreck

268 **orbèd continent** the sun

273 **durance** imprisonment

275 **enlarge** free

277 **distract** mentally disturbed

281–2 **Beelzebub ... end** the devil at bay

284 **epistles** letters

skills not doesn't matter

293 **vox** the appropriate voice

296 **perpend** pay attention

316 **proper** own

318 **quits you** releases you from service

330 **from it** differently

331 **invention** composition

333 **honour** reputation

334 **lights** signs, indications

337 **lighter** lesser

341 **geck** fool

344 **character** handwriting

348 **presupposed** previously suggested

350 **passed** been passed, played

359 **Upon** because of

361 **importance** importunity

363 **pluck on** induce

367 **baffled** disgraced

374 **whirligig** spinning top

379 **convents** calls together

400 **tosspots** drunkards

Part three

CRITICAL APPROACHES

CHARACTERISATION

Characters in a play are just that: characters. It may seem obvious to say that they are not real people and that they should not be discussed as such. They consist of what they say and what is said about them: they are composed of words, not flesh and blood, nor of inner psychology. It is significant that the very word 'character' derives from words denoting marking or writing (as in its use in *Twelfth Night* at V.1.344, when Olivia is describing the counterfeit handwriting in Malvolio's letter), only gaining its predominant modern meanings of 'individual personality' or 'person in a play' in the late seventeenth century. Sometimes Shakespearean characters have a representative, rather than an individual function: they embody behaviours or characteristics as symbolic personifications. Sometimes naming can be a clue to this: the name 'Feste', for example, derives from the Latin *festivus* = a feast, the **etymology** and associations of Sir Toby Belch are rather cruder. Some characters exist as dramatic devices rather than as fully realised individuals – Fabian's role is plot-based, rather than psychological. At other times, Shakespeare's gift for recognisable and distinctive characterisation is evident: single phrases or gestures can suggest an entire personality (such as Sir Andrew Aguecheek's pensive 'I was adored once, too' (II.3.174)). In performance the assumptions of the **Method** school tend to dominate, whereby the inner motivations of the characters – their life beyond what is written for them in the play – are a crucial part of directors' and actors' interpretation. These notes on characters use information from modern performances where it offers a particular slant, but they also try to remember that Shakespeare's characters derive from an age in which personality and the sense of the individual were quite different from now, and especially that they are part of a theatrical culture in which **verisimilitude** was not always the prime concern. When Fabian remarks knowingly that 'If this were played upon a stage now, I could condemn it as an improbable fiction' (III.4.126–7), he is revealing, rather than hiding, the artificiality of events (see Background, on Shakespeare's Theatre).

VIOLA

The Oscar-winning film *Shakespeare in Love* (1998) ends with Shakespeare beginning to write *Twelfth Night* after the Lady Viola, with whom he has had a passionate affair, has left London with her husband. There's no evidence at all that Viola, or indeed any Shakespearean character, is based on the author's direct experience, but this device at the end of the film does attest to the vitality generations of readers and theatregoers have found in the character of Viola. Writing in the eighteenth century, Samuel Johnson described her as 'a cunning schemer, never at a loss'; the opposite view was taken by the critic William Hazlitt, who wrote in 1817 that she is 'the great and secret charm' of the play: 'much as we like cakes and ale there is something that we like better' (see Critical History & Broader Perspectives).

We first encounter Viola when she is cast up on the shore of Illyria, believing her twin Sebastian lost in the shipwreck. Throughout the play she is a stranger in a potentially inhospitable land, but, amid her grief, she shows courage and resourcefulness in deciding to dress as a boy and enter the service of Orsino. In III.4 she admits that she has consciously adopted Sebastian's appearance, and it may be that her disguise is a way of keeping her brother alive until their eventual reunion in Act V. In productions she often borrows his clothing from a chest saved from the wreck. Like Olivia (their names are virtual anagrams, signalling that they are made up of similar elements but in a different order) it seems she has recently lost her father and, she fears, her brother; unlike Olivia she does not respond to loss by retreating into herself, but gives her situation up to the restorative powers of 'time' (II.2.40).

Zoë Wanamaker, who played Viola at the Royal Shakespeare Theatre in 1983–4, described her character as 'the catalyst of the play' who enters the 'locked-up stillness of Illyria' to bring 'life, and chaos, and hope', 'stirring up the place, forcing them all up into a spiral'. Viola is certainly associated with movement throughout the play: she is the go-between for Orsino to Olivia and moves between their households, she has individual conversations with Olivia, Orsino, Malvolio, Feste and Sebastian and, as such, is the major connective force between the different characters and plot strands. Her arrival breaks up the stalemate of Orsino's extravagant and unrequited love for Olivia, and equally dismantles the sterility of Olivia's self-imposed mourning. As Cesario she is able to challenge Orsino's glib sexism about women's inability to love: 'there is no woman's sides / Can bide the beating of so strong a passion / As love doth give my heart' (II.4.92–4), with her own heartfelt 'We men … prove / Much in our vows, but little in our love' (II.4.115–17). She is also able to identify Olivia's pride (I.5.239), and thus reintroduce her to the world she has ignored.

For all her conversations – swapping witticisms with Feste, parrying Olivia's passionate questioning, at once evading and confessing to Orsino – Viola is in some sense alone for much of the play, unable to open up to anybody because of the disguise she calls 'a wickedness' (II.2.27). She has no confidante other than the audience, although the relative lack of **soliloquies** or **asides** addressed to the audience suggests that she does not really confide in us either. Her encounters with Orsino and Olivia are emotionally charged, but there is the constant echo of what must remain unspoken. Her love for Orsino is ventriloquised as the 'willow cabin' she would, were she he, build at Olivia's gate (I.5.257), or as the pining passion of her ill-fated imaginary sister who, like Viola herself, 'never told her love, / But let concealment, like a worm i' the bud, / Feed on her damask cheek' (II.4.109–11). Her love can only be voiced in a kind of disguise, dressed as something or someone else, in an emotional and linguistic parallel to her physical disguise as Cesario.

Frequently she alludes to the disparity between her real self and the part she is playing: 'I am not what I play' (I.5.177), she tells Olivia at their first meeting, and by the second, the gap between appearance and reality has become wider and more profound: 'I am not what I am' (III.1.136). Viola's self-expression can only come out in riddles and evasions and projections, and when she is apparently closest to the man she loves her disguise pushes her beyond reach. Helen Schlesinger, another RSC Viola, in 1997–8, found in her character an 'elusive' quality, describing it as 'a very lonely part. There's a bit of her that is always hidden', and this oblique aspect of Viola might be thought to remain even at the play's conclusion when the return of her woman's clothing keeps being referred to but never actually happens. Strikingly, for viewers of the play in the theatre (as opposed to readers of the text), she is never given her name until the last scene: until Sebastian greets her 'Thrice welcome, drownèd Viola' (V.1.238) she does not attain the individual identity denoted by her forename. Thereafter she speaks her own name twice in ten lines, including the decisive assertion of self 'I am Viola' (line 250). There is a sense, therefore, in which she is not a complete person until she is reunited with her twin at the play's conclusion (Orsino, significantly, continues to call her 'Cesario' to the end). In Trevor Nunn's film of the play, the shipwreck is shown in great detail, including an underwater shot of Viola and Sebastian being riven apart by the swirling current: it has **metaphorical** associations of the amniotic fluid of the womb, associating the shipwreck with a kind of birth trauma separating the two twins and therefore suggesting that the whole play is an attempt to return to that privileged togetherness they enjoyed before birth. Perhaps the play's symbolic resolution can therefore be seen as located in the twins' reunion rather than in the final double marriages.

ORSINO

Orsino's famous declaration of love opens the play: 'If music be the food of love, play on' (I.1.1). He is thus immediately established as a lover of extravagant proportions, indulging his **hyperbolic** passion for a woman who has made it repeatedly clear she does not want anything to do with him. He does not seem to know Olivia as an individual: instead, his language is full of romance clichés and preoccupied with the exquisite masochism of unrequited love: 'my desires, like fell and cruel hounds, / E'er since pursue me' (I.1.24–5). Orsino's love is thoroughly self-absorbed. He is more concerned with himself as lover than with the ostensible object of his love, thus suggesting he is narcissistic. In the opening scene he imagines that he will eventually be 'one self king' (I.1.40) of Olivia's affections, suggesting a marital hierarchy rather than mutuality.

    It is from this egotism that Viola is able to nudge him. Telling the story of her 'sister' she wrests his attention from his own preoccupations and alerts his attention from his love for Olivia to the possibility of female love (II.4) (see Textual Analysis, Text 2). From this emotional scene in which she disguises her love for him and plants the suggestion that his view of women is inadequate and restricted, he does not appear again until the end of the play. By this time, his emotional reliance on Cesario has eclipsed his love for Olivia, so that when he mistakenly believes they are married, his hurt and sense of betrayal falls not on his worshipped mistress but on his 'page': 'this your minion, whom I know you love, / And whom, by heaven, I swear, I tender dearly, / Him will I tear out of that cruel eye / Where he sits crownèd in his master's spite' (V.1.123–6). The proposed marriage between Cesario and Olivia shocks Orsino into a declaration of love, but not this time the conventional and self-indulgent phrases of his love for Olivia, but a vigorous, passionate, violent desire for 'Cesario': 'I'll sacrifice the lamb that I do love' (V.1.129).

Through Viola's disguise, she and Orsino have discussed many topics. They have got to know each other before recognising each other as lovers. Orsino responds quickly and openly to the newcomer: 'Thou knowest no less but all. I have unclasped / To thee the book even of my secret soul' (I.4.13–14). There is, however, a lingering sense that it was the boy Cesario Orsino fell in love with, and his final words to his bride stress the homoerotic foundations of their relationship: 'Cesario, come; / For so you shall be, while you are a man' (V.1.382–3). Trevor Nunn's film drew attention to this aspect of the growing rapport between the Duke and his feminine page, so that when Viola and Orsino listen together to Feste's song in II.4, they find themselves gradually leaning towards each other as if to kiss, then Orsino starts backwards, shocked at his own attraction to this young man. For this Orsino, the revelation of Cesario's femininity was less a shock than a relief, in explaining that his feelings of desire were heterosexual after all. Their relationship, however, contributes to the sexually ambiguous undertones of the play's many depictions of love (see Themes, on Love & Self-love, and Critical History & Broader Perspectives).

OLIVIA

We hear a good deal about Olivia before she appears on stage – Orsino, the sea captain, Sir Toby, Sir Andrew, Maria and Feste all mention her before her first entrance in I.5. This extended introduction is entirely suitable for a character who is at the centre of so many different people's desires and perceptions: the idealising love of Orsino and Sir Andrew, neither of whom ever speak directly to her until the last scene, the self-serving ambitions of Malvolio, the freeloading of Sir Toby, and the **satiric** wit of Feste. Each of these characters has a different idea of what lies behind the veil of her mourning. The veil is an appropriate symbol: perhaps we never really know what motivates this woman who first eschews the world and love and then quickly falls for a young page who comes to visit her, who marries in haste but seems unperturbed (or at least does not respond) by her new husband's revelation that she is 'betrothed both to a maid and a man' (V.1.260). Her urgent desire for Cesario is deflected into marriage with Sebastian, but it is not clear whether the outward similarity between her desired and her actual partner will be enough: essentially, she marries a man because he looks like a woman she fell in love with, which may not be an altogether happy start for a marriage. Some critics have argued that this marriage based on a misapprehension is a kind of punishment for Olivia's excessive behaviour at the opening of the play: a woman who refuses to be a part of 'normal' social and family life, preferring the love of a dead brother to that of an ardent new suitor, is disciplined by being made to humiliate herself in pursuit of a woman and then to marry a stranger. On the other hand, Olivia herself likens the rapidity of her love for Cesario to the catching the 'plague' (I.5.284); she is lucky, perhaps, to escape from this dangerous condition with a suitable husband.

Feste

Perhaps Feste is less a character than a function. His is a **choric**, commentary role, rather than a participatory one. At the RSC in 1979, he remained on stage throughout the play, cueing characters' entrances like a kind of stage-manager. His strength comes from his observation: 'He must observe their mood on whom he jests, / ... This is a practise / As full of labour as a wise man's art' (Viola, III.1.60–4). Perhaps, as Cesario suggests in III.1, he knows more than he is letting on: Trevor Nunn's film of the play had Feste, played by Ben Kingsley, watching from the clifftop as Viola made her way up the beach and made it clear that he alone sees through Cesario's disguise. He may be an older man: having been fool to Olivia's father, he provides a link with her family history which has been so fractured by the recent and traumatic deaths of her father and brother.

Stephen Boxer, who played the role for the RSC in 1997–8, described the importance of language to Feste: 'Some of the more obscure

meanings you can make clear by vocal tricks and gesture. He creates his
own language – not necessarily sense in the way that other characters
speak but an anarchic kind of sense'. It is through his verbal dexterity that
Feste expresses his own oblique perspective on the events of the play: 'I
am indeed not her fool, but her corrupter of words' (III.1.34–5). Feste's
unique position in the play as an 'allowed fool' (I.5.89) gives him the
freedom to speak his own enigmatic form of wisdom. In a play
preoccupied with who is the fool – Feste **puns** on this in his first scene
with Olivia, responding to her exasperated 'Take the fool away' with 'Do
you not hear, fellows? Take away the lady' (I.5.34–5) – he embodies the
disinterested clarity denied to the other characters who are too wrapped
up in the unfolding plot. As Viola observes, 'This fellow is wise enough
to play the fool' (III.1.58). His role is to point out the truths other
characters do not want to hear: the grief-stricken Olivia that her brother
is in heaven and therefore beyond mourning; the carousing Sir Toby that
he lies when he speaks of his own immortality (II.3.103); Orsino, who is
boasting male constancy, that he is as changeable as the opal (II.4.74);
Cesario that he wants a beard (III.1.44). His is a wit that is always tinged
with melancholy: his songs reverberate with ageing, death and with
winter weather. It is hardly surprising that the song with which he ends
the play crops up again in Shakespeare's bleakest tragedy, *King Lear*.

Feste, however, drops his disengaged stance in the baiting of
Malvolio. The two represent opposed polarities: the anarchic and the
methodical; the irreverent and the sycophantic; the spender and the
hoarder. Perhaps Malvolio touches a nerve in his acidic observation at
their first encounter in the play: 'unless you laugh and minister occasion
to him, he is gagged' (I.5.81–2); Feste refers again to it in V.1, so the
insult has not been forgotten: 'an you smile not, he's gagged' (line 373).
Like any professional comedian, Feste needs the approval of an audience:
without that, he is as good as gagged. Malvolio's refusal to play along is
the source of Feste's implacable hostility, and we see the fool's disinterest
turn to cruelty in his disguise as Sir Topas.

Malvolio

John Manningham's account of an early performance of *Twelfth Night*
takes particular delight in the Malvolio plot (see Note on the Text), and

this enjoyment has been an ongoing feature in audience responses to the play on the stage. The spectacle of the gullible, aspirant, hypocritical steward made to look a fool by those he has humiliated seems to appeal to spectators, both on- and off-stage. There are, however, two ways to look at Malvolio's entry in II.3. An unsympathetic interpretation would see Malvolio as a party-pooper, the self-righteous voice of the early-to-bed when faced with revellers, a man who enjoys his moral superiority over his social superiors. According to this reading, Malvolio's own pomposity sets him up for his mortification, and the rapidity with which he is persuaded that Olivia loves him attests to his social-climbing self-delusion. If Malvolio is seen in a more positive light, however, we might think that he is only doing his job as the conscientious steward of a household that is still in mourning and in which, therefore, loud revelry is most inappropriate. In this light it is Sir Toby and the others who are in the wrong, and Malvolio is the victim of his own diligence. There is some support for this second view in Olivia's concern for her seemingly mad steward: 'I would not have him miscarry for the half of my dowry' (III.4.63–4). Clearly she relies on Malvolio to manage her household.

Many productions have attempted to suggest that Malvolio is a hypocrite. In Trevor Nunn's film he is shown reading a salacious French magazine. The alacrity and clarity with which he imagines himself husband to Olivia show that he is not so puritanical as he might seem: his mind tends towards fantasies of sex ('having come from a day-bed, where I have left Olivia sleeping' II.5.47–8), material possessions ('wind up my watch or play with my – some rich jewel', lines 59–60), and power ('I extend my hand to him thus – quenching my familiar smile with an austere regard of control', lines 65–6). The preposterous vision of his acting out these fantasies in the orchard establishes him as an inflated individual who needs to be taken down a notch. Having said that, however, we may well feel that the joke against him goes too far (see Themes, on Twelfth Night). When Nigel Hawthorne as Malvolio reappears at the end of Nunn's film, dishevelled and trying desperately to put his toupee straight, the sense is of a man denied any dignity at all, and of a humiliation from which he cannot recover. His last words are an explicit threat, discordant among the marriages and explanations and reconciliations that characterise the final scene, as his implacable hostility to Feste and his tormentors remains: 'I'll be revenged on the whole pack of you' (V.1.375). Philip Voss, who took on the role at the RSC in 1997, described his interpretation of Malvolio's last exit: 'At the end I want to howl and point to heaven – I shall try to pull up my socks and leave with dignity. I would like the audience to be heartbroken by him and to feel embarrassed. They must laugh, but then feel embarrassed'. Michael Pennington's view is harsher: 'he goes, darkness closing like a tide behind him. I think there is a pause, nobody quite knows what to do'. Malvolio's revenge upsets the play's comic resolution.

Certainly Malvolio is thoroughly punished. While he is not alone in 'self-love' (I.5.85) – this is a feature of Orsino and Olivia's behaviour too – he is disciplined and humiliated for this failing, rather than, as they are, educated out of it through love. He is not alone in aspiring to an apparently unreachable love object either: Viola, Olivia, Antonio and Orsino all do this to some degree, and Maria, another household employee, eventually does marry far above her social station. The extent of Malvolio's punishment, then, makes him seem like a scapegoat, bearing the displaced penalty of the failings of the whole cast. His role suggests the cruelty inherent in comedy: the sour taste left after 'what you will' (See Themes, on Twelfth Night).

SIR TOBY

Is Sir Toby a plump and genial *bon viveur*, the embodiment of the carnival spirit of excess and self-gratification, or is he a freeloader, sponging off his niece and off his companion Sir Andrew? As with Malvolio, his opposite (in productions they are often physically opposed types, with Toby fat from indulgence and Malvolio thin and pinched), there are two ways to see his character, but unlike Malvolio, audiences have generally been sympathetic to this profligate, humorous and self-indulgent rogue described by director Michael Pennington as 'deadly fun, completely without morals, articulate, witty and full-blooded'. It's been suggested that in the characterisation of Sir Toby Belch, Shakespeare was trying to recreate his most successful comic conception, the fat and disreputable knight of the *Henry IV* plays, Falstaff. One actor who has played Sir Toby, however, argued that the jollity was all a case of over-compensation for a man who has also lost a nephew (Olivia's dead brother) and, like Olivia and Viola, a brother in Olivia's father.

Sometimes Sir Toby has been played as a man having one last fling before hanging up his drinking boots and settling into a more respectable old age, hence, perhaps, Feste's pointed references to time passing in the drinking scene. Seen in this light, his marriage to Maria is part of the 'last chance' mood (see Themes, on Twelfth Night).

Notwithstanding the general affection for Sir Toby outside the play, he shows little regard for anyone else in the play. His first words criticise Olivia for her mourning, and his last ones disparage Sir Andrew. There are flashes of friction between him and Feste. His wooing of Maria is a largely off-stage business, and the admiration he expresses for her is linked firmly with her plotting against Malvolio. He rejects decisively Maria's suggestion that 'you must confine yourself within the modest limits of order' (I.3.7–8): confinement, modesty and order are antipathetic to Toby's excessive and disorderly conduct (See Themes, on Twelfth Night; Excess). Almost all his scenes involve drinking and singing, and he rejects the authority of clock-time and perhaps, by extension, of the limitation of time itself. His habitually elevated diction – words such as 'cubiculo' (III.2.50) and 'encounter' (III.1.72) – suggests a man of learning but also one with an **ironic**, self-conscious approach to proceedings. His motivations are sometimes difficult to discern: in the matter of the duel between Sir Andrew and Cesario, for example, he seems merely to enjoy the spectacle of these reluctant swordsmen, telling each party blood-curdling stories of the other's merciless valour.

SIR ANDREW

Sir Andrew's role in the last twenty-five or so lines of II.5 symbolises his role throughout the play. Here his words echo Sir Toby's: he seems to have no voice or opinions of his own, but is merely a paler shadow of his robust companion. Sir Andrew also shadows Orsino: his comically unrequited wooing of Olivia – the two are never on stage at the same time until after Olivia's marriage – is a fainter version of Orsino's passion. When Andrew and Cesario are at the point of duelling, the spectacle is of two unmanly opponents: the effeminate Sir Andrew and the disguised Viola. Sir Andrew is repeatedly characterised as a fool who does not understand French, who misunderstands words and uses them wrongly (as at I.3.49–50), who must borrow wooing terms from a page

(III.1.87–8), whose masculinity is in question (Maria's **pun** on 'dry' suggests impotence at I.3.70). On the stage his ineffectual demeanour is often amplified by added stage business: Trevor Nunn's film shows him in slapstick sequences, including crashing through the glass of a greenhouse; often he is shown unwittingly wearing yellow until he learns it is Olivia's least favourite colour. There is, though, a hint of pathos, a past life lost, in his wistful words 'I was adored once, too' (II.3.174).

SEBASTIAN

Almost all that matters about Sebastian in the play is that he looks like Viola, or, perhaps more precisely, that he looks like Cesario. Since his major purpose is to be like someone else, therefore, it is perhaps not surprising that he has little strength of personality himself. He is a virtual cipher, a plot function, a way of untying the knots into which the play has tangled itself. Although he attracts strong feelings from a sister who believes he is dead, from a seaman who saved him from the ocean and will sacrifice anything for him, from a woman who marries him as soon as she claps eyes on him, in his own person he is rather insignificant, appearing in only four scenes. His first entrance shows him bemoaning 'the malignancy of my fate' (II.1.4), mourning his sister 'with salt water' (line 27); he seems hardly to notice the doglike devotion of Antonio. In his second scene, he expresses his gratitude for Antonio's company, and proposes, perhaps rather callowly, that they do some sightseeing. His questions of Antonio about the precise nature of his offence against Orsino's sailors might also reveal a kind of immaturity. Sebastian is performing his own deeds of derring-do in his next scene, the fight with Sir Andrew when he is mistaken for Cesario, in which he breaks the hapless knight's head. Here he meets Olivia, and is entranced by her kindness to him, believing himself asleep but agreeing to be 'ruled' by her (IV.1.63). His entrance into the final scene of the play is as 'the very devil incarnate' (V.1.178–9) who has wounded Sir Toby and Sir Andrew. He greets Antonio warmly: 'How have the hours racked and tortured me / Since I have lost thee!' (lines 216–17). His reunion with Viola is slower, more halting in their mutual rediscovery: his last words to Olivia are the rueful 'You are betrothed both to a maid and a man' (line 260): there is no further conversation between or about them which would give any clue about how she has taken this news. Sebastian's insubstantiality is an inevitable function of his role in the plot.

ANTONIO

Alone of all the characters in the play, Antonio knows whom he loves, articulates that love, and acts selflessly because of it. He risks himself to follow Sebastian into Illyria; he freely gives him his money to buy some souvenir or gewgaw; he offers to take on himself the duel he believes Sebastian to be engaged in with Sir Andrew. His actions are all prompted by his affection, expressed in brief **soliloquy**: 'I do adore thee so' (II.1.42). It's striking, therefore, that he remains outside the charmed circle of couples at the end of the play: once Sebastian has been reunited with Viola he spares not a word for his protector, who is almost forgotten in the general celebrations and explanations. Many productions have chosen to suggest that Antonio's love is not platonic but sexual, and certainly the vehemence of his feelings gives strength to this interpretation. This hint of homoeroticism combines with the ambiguous sexuality of Orsino's intimacy with his page Cesario and Olivia's love for Viola-disguised-as-Cesario (see Critical History & Broader Perspectives). Whether or not Antonio is homosexual (the term itself is anachronistic in relation to the Elizabethan period), his is a role characterised by self-sacrificing love for a man who seems scarcely to register, let alone earn, this devotion.

THEMES

TWELFTH NIGHT, OR WHAT YOU WILL

The play is almost unique among Shakespeare's works in having a double title, and this might be seen to introduce the theme of doubling or duplication from the outset – a theme that has other expressions in the two households of Orsino and Olivia, the motif of the twins, and the relationship between the almost anagrammatical Olivia and Viola, each of whom mourns a dead brother and father.

The play's first title, *Twelfth Night*, refers of course to the feast of the Epiphany or 6 January, the final day of the Christmas festivities. Since there is no explicit reference to this time of year within the play, scholars have argued, following Leslie Hotson's book on the play published in 1954, that it was first performed on this occasion in 1601. This is neat, but unsubstantiated: there is no real evidence that the play was first performed, or written, for the Twelfth Night celebrations.

Samuel Pepys, the seventeenth-century diarist and theatregoer, didn't think much of *Twelfth Night*, noting that it was 'not relating at all to the name or the day'. Pepys is, though, wrong in this. Twelfth Night, like other Elizabethan festivals, was marked by licensed misrule, by the topsy-turvy inversion of normal social relationships symbolised in the festival title of 'Lord of Misrule' (Sir Toby, perhaps?). Sometimes such festivals involved servants being waited on by their masters, or men wearing women's clothes or being ruled by their wives – Orsino's description of Cesario as her 'master's mistress' (V.1.323) fits in with these images of disorder. Viola's adoption of male clothing can also be seen in this festival context. The play has an unreal quality of pretence: it is full of unlikely coincidences and interrelations appropriate to a time when normal rules and behaviours are suspended. The play does mention other festivals, although not Twelfth Night itself: Olivia judges Malvolio's behaviour 'midsummer madness' (III.4.56) and Fabian talks about the farcical duel preparations of Sir Andrew and Cesario as 'matter for a May morning' (III.4.141). Eating and drinking are a major part of the plot with Sir Toby (see Themes, on Excess). If II.3, the drinking scene with Sir Toby and Sir Andrew carousing into the night, represents the spirit of festival or carnival, then Malvolio is an anti-festival figure, a killjoy, whose punishment ultimately defends the right to enjoy 'cakes and ale' (II.3.112). His punishment, being imprisoned in a dark room, is the ultimate and terrifying experience of endless winter.

But Twelfth Night is not only a festival, it is a culmination of the days of merrymaking marking Christmas. It represents the end of things. It is the last day of feasting and merriment before normal life, self-denial, winter darkness and the old regulations set in. It is the day when the Christmas decorations come down and the house suddenly looks bare. Shakespeare's play picks up the elegiac, wistful associations of the end of the festival period. There is a sense of the clock ticking, of a limit to the festival world, of normal life waiting in the wings, even a sense of urgency about the revelry. The play closes not on the image of the two newly formed couples but on Feste, the distinctly unfestive clown. The RSC director Terry Hands took this as the keynote of his 1979 production: 'the festive moment has passed, and this is now the cruellest point of the year'. He saw II.3 as the wretched attempt of the revellers to recapture the spirit of the festival, trying 'to put their Christmas tree back up'. Feste's final glum song stresses that 'the rain it raineth every day' (V.1.389): the realities of winter weather cannot be shut out of the party, and the play ends on a note of resolution but also of melancholy. The play's references to cold, such as the image of the unrequited lover 'hang[ing] like an icicle on a Dutchman's beard' (III.2.26) cannot be entirely banished by the warm glow of its romantic ending. If the play has provided its audience with an umbrella against this intemperate climate, it is clearly stated in the terms of the loan that it, like the midwinter festival itself, is only temporary.

This sense of the festivities coming to a close can also be traced through the play's references to time. There is a sense of hurry, even a desperation, about Olivia's marriage to Sebastian, which she acknowledges but does not explain in her 'Blame not this haste of mine' (IV.3.22). She seems to need to seize the moment, as if it might not ever recur. It is the clock striking that changes her attitude to Cesario in III.1: 'The clock upbraids me with the waste of time' (III.1.127), perhaps referring not only to the current interview but to the length of her mourning and the sense of time passing and lost for ever (see Textual Analysis, Text 3). Sir Toby's attempt to defy the clock and extend the party through the night also has an air of impotent rebellion about it, skewered neatly by Feste's unflinching song: 'Youth's a stuff will not endure' (III.1.50) and his reply to Sir Toby's 'But I will never die': 'Sir Toby, there you lie' (lines 103–4). Old age and its symbolic counterpart, winter, are never far beneath the surface in *Twelfth Night*.

If *Twelfth Night* has a sense of its own revels ending, it also forms an ending of Shakespeare's own period of writing romantic comedy. During the 1590s romantic comedy ending in marriage and harmony was a major part of Shakespeare's repertoire, whereas the first decade of the seventeenth century was to be characterised by an intense focus on tragedy (see Background, on Shakespeare's Dramatic Career). Even Malvolio's parting words of revenge (V.1.375) look forward to another kind of play with an altogether different mood – the tragedies on which Shakespeare was to concentrate for the next decade. Perhaps this sense of

Twelfth Night as his last comedy also adds a note of wistfulness to the revels. Put this way, it seems that it is Malvolio who has ultimately triumphed at the end, despite his personal humiliation.

If 'Twelfth Night' suggests festivity, but more insistently the end of festivity with the associations of winter and old age, the play's subtitle, 'What You Will', gives a different slant to interpretations of the play. Shakespeare enjoyed **punning** on the word 'will', including on his own name, particularly in his **sonnets**, and the phrase here could be paraphrased in a number of ways: what you want, what you would like, what you desire, what you please, whatever you want, over to you, have it your way, so you say, anything goes. Any of these could be applied to the play's characters, who 'will' themselves into new identities and new possibilities: Viola as Cesario, Olivia as a wife, Orsino out of masochistic love, Malvolio as Count, Sir Andrew as a fierce dueller. The phrase also poses an insouciant sort of challenge to us as readers or audience: we can do what we want with the play, it's up to us. We have to take some responsibility. Our laughter supported the initial gulling of Malvolio, but maybe things did go too far. Like the cautionary fairy tales which warn how problematic it is to have our wishes granted, the play suggests that what we will may not always turn out to be what we thought, and so the play simultaneously questions and indulges some of our fantasies.

EXCESS

Related to the theme of 'Twelfth Night' is the theme of excess. At the RSC production in 1997, the stage was dominated by an enormous oversized fridge for late-night raids by Sir Toby. This was an apt visual symbol for his gluttony and self-indulgence, but excess is not only a matter of eating and drinking in the play. From Orsino's desire for 'excess' of music (I.1.2) to the arguably excessive length of Olivia's mourning, from Malvolio 'sick' of excessive self-love (I.5.85) to the 'extravagancy' of Sebastian's voyage (II.1.10), the play is preoccupied with immoderate passions. These excesses are, for the most part, moderated or brought into line by the end of the play: Orsino is educated about the real nature of women by his conversations with Cesario and into a love based on the intimacy of companionship rather than idealisation from afar; Olivia is jolted out of her sterile dependence on her dead male relatives into sudden passionate love; Malvolio is humiliated for his presumption in believing Olivia in love with him. It seems that the play endorses Maria's suggestion to Sir Toby, that he 'confine [himself] within the modest limits of order' (I.3.7–8), as immoderate desire is regulated in the triple marriages with which *Twelfth Night* concludes.

LOVE & SELF-LOVE

Comedies are generally about courtship leading to marriage, but *Twelfth Night* shows a number of variations on the theme of love, particularly around the difference between selfish and selfless love. Orsino's initial passion for Olivia seems based more on an idea of himself as a lover than on an acknowledgement of her separateness as a loved one. In turning from Olivia to Viola in the final scene, he shows how he has been educated out of narcissistic infatuation and into a relationship based on mutual intimacy. Another reading of this final marriage, however, would stress that this apparent intimacy between Orsino and Viola is not the intimacy of heterosexual lovers but an unusual closeness between master and servant, and that, far from registering real knowledge of each other, this suggests that their relationship is based on misrecognition. Olivia's commitment to mourning also seems a kind of self-love, out of which she is shaken by her sudden love for Cesario. Perhaps the extremity of her passion for this youth and her humiliating misinterpretation of 'his' outward appearance – clearly, physical looks are a large part of her attraction to 'him – is a kind of punishment, analogous to that of Malvolio but ultimately more benign, for her narcissism. She too, however, does not marry the person she thought, unless we are to believe that a play so sceptical about outward appearances means us to think that Sebastian and Viola are indeed essentially interchangeable. Malvolio's self-love is commented on by Olivia, and he is soundly punished for his self-regard and for his readiness to believe that 'my lady loves me' (II.5.159). Sir Toby reports that Maria 'adores' him (II.3.172); Sir Andrew's ineffectual suit of Olivia seems to have little passion in it although he does report that he, too, 'was adored once' (II.3.174). Feste's songs in II.3 – 'O mistress mine' and 'What is love' – provide a more cynical view of love, and one that is tied inexorably to suffering. He tells of a lover 'slain by a fair cruel maid' (II.4.53) amid the scene between

Orsino and Viola in which they discuss the different properties of men's and women's love. Orsino argues that no woman could bear the 'beating of so strong a passion / As love doth give my heart' (II.4.93–4); Viola counters with a vehement defence of women's silent constancy, displacing her own situation on to her patient sister who 'never told her love' (line 109). It is striking, however, that the one constant, selfless love, that of Antonio for Sebastian, cannot find a place in the general rejoicing at the end of the play. It is not part of the relentless move towards heterosexual marriage, so that Antonio, like Malvolio and Feste, remains outside the celebrations.

Ultimately, perhaps the most profound symbol of love as the union of two persons into one is the reunited twins, Viola and Sebastian. So alike that they are like a 'division' of one, 'An apple cleft in twain' (V.1.219–20) – and Shakespeare, as the father of boy-girl twins himself (see Background, on Shakespeare's Life) must have known that this was very unlikely to be literally true – they represent the union of souls. Platonic theory held that everyone had lost part of themselves and that life was a search for that missing part: Sebastian and Viola's miraculous reunion represents the reuniting of a single self, rather than the meeting of distinct individuals. The gradual awestruck realisation of what each scarcely dares believe could be true (V.1.222–50) is a more profound coming together than the rather perfunctory proposal of marriage by Orsino to Viola, or the mistaken identities that prompt Olivia's marriage to Orsino.

GENDER

On the Elizabethan stage, Viola would have been played by a boy actor – there were no women actors on the public stage until the Restoration in 1660 (see Background, on Shakespeare's Theatre). Many of Shakespeare's comedies, including *Two Gentlemen of Verona*, *As You Like It* and *The Merchant of Venice* play on this fact. Our own visual images of men dressed as women may be misleading in trying to imagine the effects of this dramatic convention. It is thought that these boy actors must have been extremely good and extremely convincing as women, but still, the awareness that underneath this role was a male body must have been prominent. Rather than suppressing or ignoring this physical fact,

Shakespeare seems to enjoy playing on the confusions it engenders (**pun intended**). Many recent critics have discussed whether Shakespeare's use of cross-dressed heroines within the context of all-male acting companies is ultimately conservative or radical in its attitude to gender roles (see Critical History & Broader Perspectives). Does Viola's intimacy with Orsino gained through her disguise suggest that the conventions about courtship are foolish restriction, or does the fact that she uses her disguise as a man to pursue romance – the 'feminine' sphere – rather than something more challenging to masculine authority actually reinforce gender conventions?

Viola's disguise can be read to suggest that women's roles are over-circumscribed by gender convention, and that genuine affection cannot flourish in such artificial confines. By being a man with Orsino she is really able to get to know him on more like equal terms and to be sure of her love for him. Certainly Orsino and Cesario become intimate through the freedom offered by her disguise. Whereas Olivia remains for Orsino a remote ideal (he doesn't even do his wooing in person, preferring to send a servant), Cesario/Viola quickly becomes a trusted confidant. In the Trevor Nunn film, this intimacy tips into sexual attraction, and we watch Orsino struggling with his feelings as he cannot believe he fancies a young boy. Viola's revelation at the end of the play comes as a great relief to him and, now she is a woman, he can indulge his feelings for her – or him. Much of the humour in performance can derive from the play's repeated flirtation with an apparently homosexual attraction which, in the end, it realigns with the conventions of heterosexual romantic comedy. It is a play fascinated with sexual possibilities, and in this respect it is strikingly modern: a woman falls in love with a character we know to be a woman, and a man falls in love with a character he believes to be a man – and it milks these situations for comedy before sorting everything out like Noah's ark.

Perhaps the success of Viola's disguise suggests that gender identity is in the eye of the beholder – a man is someone recognised as and treated as a man, rather than a biological specimen in possession of a certain configuration of organs. This is a radical thought: in a society like Elizabethan England, in which the superiority of the male and the inferiority of the female was a cultural given, taking on male clothing and with it male authority could be rather challenging. Perhaps Viola's disguise tests the boundaries of gender, rather than kowtowing to them. As Diana Rigg, who played Viola in 1966 commented later: 'I think the really clever thing that Shakespeare posed ... is a sexuality which is not based on the extremes of feminism or masculinism that we have nowadays'. Other of Shakespeare's cross-dressed heroines such as *As You Like It*'s Rosalind or Portia in *The Merchant of Venice* re-establish their femininity at the end of the play by returning in their female clothes, but not so Viola. There are several references in the final scene to her 'masculine usurped attire' (V.1.247), 'maiden weeds' (V.1.252), 'woman's weeds' (V.1.270) and 'maid's garments' (V.1.272), but the sea captain never returns with them. As Orsino observes in his closing remarks: 'Cesario come; / For so you shall be, while you are a man. / But when in other habits you are seen – / Orsino's mistress and his fancy's queen' (V.2.382–5). In refusing to readmit a feminine Viola at its conclusion, the play seems reluctant to relinquish its festivity, the social and sexual topsy-turvy of carnival (See Themes, on Twelfth Night).

MADNESS

The words 'mad', 'madness' and 'madman' together appear around forty times in the play, and this frequency registers its preoccupation with the topic. As events spiral into bewilderment, characters revert to the only apparent explanation for this irrationality: madness. Feste tells Olivia that Sir Toby's drunkenness makes him 'a madman' (I.5.126); Malvolio asks the revellers 'My masters, are you mad?' (II.3.85); Olivia recognises that her quick love for Cesario is a kind of 'madness' making her 'as mad as he [Malvolio]' (III.4.14–15); Sebastian wonders if he is 'mad' when Olivia addresses him so fondly (IV.1.60 and again at IV.3.15), and muses on whether it is in fact she who is mad (IV.3.16); Malvolio pleads with 'Sir Topas', 'do not think I am mad' (IV.2.29), and Feste continues to taunt him 'are you not mad indeed, or do you but counterfeit?' (IV.2.114–15); his letter to Olivia is signed 'the madly-used Malvolio' (V.1.307–8). Feste's habitual title for Olivia, 'madonna', seems designed to echo the word mad and its cognates, as at I.5.132–3.

    Madness is an aspect of the topsy-turvydom that governs the play (see Themes, on Twelfth Night), and related to the comedy of mistaken identities around the separated twins. In Malvolio's case, however, this

metaphorical madness, used to suggest a kind of incomprehension or irrationality, comes close to psychological breakdown, as he is pushed almost beyond sanity by the merciless Feste. As with many aspects of the play, the theme has its light, comic side but a rather darker reverse.

IMAGERY & LANGUAGE

Twelfth Night is written in a mixture of **blank verse** and prose, and it is always worth looking at the shifts between these two modes. It's been argued that Elizabethans were as subconsciously sensitive to **pentameter** cadences as we are to certain jazz or other musical rhythms, and thus that alterations in this verbal tempo would be more readily registered by Shakespeare's own audience than by modern readers. Prose is often given to speakers of lower rank or for passages of comic or bawdy exchange: it is characteristic of this division that Sir Toby Belch and Sir Andrew Aguecheek usually talk in prose, and that Malvolio follows this at his entry into their revels of II.3, whereas Malvolio speaks verse to Olivia when he pulls himself up to his full height to reassert his wounded dignity in the final act. Olivia and Viola both speak prose during I.5, but break into verse speech in the same scene and elsewhere.

The first systematic attempt to analyse Shakespeare's language is Caroline Spurgeon's book *Shakespeare's Imagery and What it Tells Us*, first published in 1935 and frequently reprinted. Spurgeon notes that the balanced language of *Twelfth Night* reflects and projects the bitter-sweet tone of the whole play. Some of the most memorable images come from the play's love poetry, such as the picture of 'Patience on a monument,/ Smiling at grief ' (II.4.113–14), but these are balanced out by robust **similes** such as Sir Andrew's limp hair hanging 'like flax on a distaff' (I.3.97). Spurgeon also notes that one of the pleasures of the play for its first audiences may well have been its high incidence of topical reference, such as Sir Toby's sheet of paper 'big enough for the bed of Ware in England' (III.2.45).

In his book *Shakespeare's Language* (Penguin, 2000), Frank Kermode discusses the importance to *Twelfth Night* of the idea of impersonation and the attempt to discriminate between what actually *is* and what *seems*. This clearly operates as a plot device, but Kermode also argues that it works on a linguistic level too. Viola's reminder to herself that she is 'not that I play' (I.5.177) infects other self-identifications, so that doubt and circumlocution seem to surround the play's characters. Olivia replies to her question 'Are you the lady of the house' in unnecessarily evasive terms, 'If I do not usurp myself, I am' (I.5.177–9). Malvolio's trick letter bears the postscript '*Thou canst not choose but know who I am*' (II.5.167); Sir Andrew's challenge addresses his assailant Cesario as 'Youth, whatsoever thou art, thou art but a scurvy fellow' (III.4.147). By means of these evasive namings and self-namings, the play's language develops the plot of mistaken identity, but it also approaches a philosophical interest in the relation between things and their names and the difficulty of language ever being truly referential. When Feste, imitating the parson, torments the imprisoned Malvolio: 'So I, being Master Parson, am Master Parson; for what is "that" but "that"? And "is" but "is"?', it is words which make Malvolio's prison and threaten to overwhelm his sense of who he is. Feste's self-confessed role as 'corruptor of words' (III.1.34–5) is, throughout, the source of his power.

PART FOUR

TEXTUAL ANALYSIS

TEXT 1   THE FIRST MEETING BETWEEN OLIVIA AND VIOLA (1.5.161–241)

VIOLA: The honourable lady of the house, which is she?

OLIVIA: Speak to me, I shall answer for her. Your will?

VIOLA: Most radiant, exquisite, and unmatchable beauty –
I pray you, tell me if this be the lady of the house, for I
never saw her. I would be loath to cast away my speech;   165
for besides that it is excellently well penned, I have
taken great pains to con it. Good beauties, let me sustain
no scorn; I am very comptible, even to the least sinister
usage.

OLIVIA: Whence came you, sir?   170

VIOLA: I can say little more than I have studied, and that
question's out of my part. Good gentle one, give me
modest assurance if you be the lady of the house, that I
may proceed in my speech.

OLIVIA: Are you a comedian?   175

VIOLA: No, my profound heart; and yet, by the very fangs
of malice, I swear I am not that I play. Are you the lady
of the house?

OLIVIA: If I do not usurp myself, I am.

VIOLA: Most certain, if you are she, you do usurp your-   180
self; for what is yours to bestow is not yours to reserve.
But this is from my commission. I will on with my
speech in your praise, and then show you the heart of
my message.

OLIVIA: Come to what is important in't. I forgive you the   185
praise.

VIOLA: Alas, I took great pains to study it, and 'tis poetical.

OLIVIA: It is the more like to be feigned; I pray you, keep it

in. I heard you were saucy at my gates, and allowed your
approach rather to wonder at you than to hear you. If   190
you be not mad, be gone; if you have reason, be brief.
'Tis not that time of moon with me, to make one in so
skipping a dialogue.

MARIA: (*showing* VIOLA *the way out*) Will you hoist sail, sir?
Here lies your way.   195

VIOLA: No, good swabber, I am to hull here a little longer.
Some mollification for your giant, sweet lady! Tell me
your mind; I am a messenger.

OLIVIA: Sure, you have some hideous matter to deliver,
when the courtesy of it is so fearful. Speak your office.   200

VIOLA: It alone concerns your ear. I bring no overture of
war, no taxation of homage. I hold the olive in my hand;
my words are as full of peace as matter.

OLIVIA: Yet you began rudely. What are you? What
would you?   205

VIOLA: The rudeness that hath appeared in me have I
learned from my entertainment. What I am and what I
would are as secret as maidenhead; to your ears divinity,
to any others profanation.

OLIVIA: Give us the place alone.   210

              MARIA *and attendants withdraw*

We will hear this divinity. Now, sir, what is your text?

VIOLA: Most sweet lady –

OLIVIA: A comfortable doctrine, and much may be said of
it. Where lies your text?

VIOLA: In Orsino's bosom.   215

OLIVIA: In his bosom! In what chapter of his bosom?

VIOLA: To answer by the method, in the first of his heart.

OLIVIA: O, I have read it; it is heresy. Have you no more to
say?

VIOLA: Good madam, let me see your face.   220

OLIVIA: Have you any commission from your lord to ne-
gotiate with my face? You are now out of your text; but
we will draw the curtain and show you the picture. Look
you, sir, such a one I was this present. Is 't not well
done?   225

VIOLA: Excellently done – if God did all.

OLIVIA: 'Tis in grain, sir, 'twill endure wind and weather.

VIOLA: 'Tis beauty truly blent, whose red and white
Nature's own sweet and cunning hand laid on.
Lady, you are the cruellest she alive   230
If you will lead these graces to the grave
And leave the world no copy.

OLIVIA: O, sir, I will not be so hard-hearted. I will give
out divers schedules of my beauty. It shall be inven-
toried, and every particle and utensil labelled to my will.   235
As, item: two lips, indifferent red; item: two grey eyes,
with lids to them; item: one neck, one chin, and so forth.
Were you sent hither to praise me?

VIOLA: I see you what you are, you are too proud,
But if you were the devil, you are fair.   240
My lord and master loves you.

This first encounter between Viola and Olivia establishes the flirtatious, mocking tone of their relationship that so beguiles Olivia. Viola enters and does not know, or affects not to know (it depends on how the scene is staged) which one of the women is Olivia. Launching into a preprepared speech of compliments with a poetic **apostrophe** – 'Most radiant, exquisite, and unmatchable beauty' (line 263) – Viola breaks off anticlimactically to check that this is indeed her intended audience. This prose interjection into her own speech deflates the romantic pretensions of Orsino's embassy, and the repeated references to the speech's artificiality as 'excellently well penned, I have taken great pains to con it' (lines 176–7), 'I took great pains to study it and 'tis poetical' (line 187) serve to undermine the message. Viola's ambivalence towards her role as surrogate wooer for the man she herself loves seems to express itself in this **ironic** undercutting of her master's words. The real irony of the situation, however, is that it is in her own voice that she is most attractive to Olivia.

Immediately, it is the messenger rather than the message that attracts Olivia. Her first response is to ask a question: 'Whence came you, sir?' (line 170). Viola turns this to her purpose by stressing that it is outside her 'part' (line 172), and a run of images drawn from acting and the theatre include Olivia's question 'Are you a comedian?' (line 175). Viola seems to be enjoying the disjunction between the role she is playing and her true self, and her hints at this discrepancy have the effect of arousing Olivia's curiosity still further. 'I am not that I play' is countered by Olivia's reply 'If I do not usurp myself, I am' (line 179): this curious response may suggest that Olivia, too, recognises a disjunction between the 'I' and the 'lady of the house' and that she sees her own dividedness echoed in this mysterious young messenger. There are many similarities between Viola and Olivia, and although these are not made explicit in the scene, it may be that their evident shared enjoyment in their conversation derives from the implicit awareness of their connections.

Throughout the scene, Viola dominates. She tends to begin verbal tricks that Olivia then picks up and returns, such as the religious connotations of 'divinity' and 'proclamation' (lines 208–9), prompting Olivia's echoing 'divinity' and 'text' (line 211). It is as if their conversation is a kind of tennis match where each player is learning the style and movement of the other. They speak in prose, suggesting a relaxed kind of intimacy, and this is stressed when Olivia dismisses Maria and her attendants. Alone with Olivia for the first time, Viola has another attempt at her set speech, but by now the ostensible reason for her audience has been overtaken, and Olivia is quickly dismissive, interrupting for the first time at line 212. The shorter to-and-fro speeches of lines 211–220 are, to continue the image of the tennis match, a quick rally which gets the heart racing, and there is an element of eroticism in Viola's invitation to Olivia to unveil herself. It's not clear why Viola should ask this.

Viola's feeling of intimacy with her interlocutor leads her to continue their joking. She speaks to her as to an equal, not in the reverential tones of an underling, and perhaps it is this freshness that so attracts Olivia. Elsewhere Orsino and Malvolio independently observe that the figure of Cesario is not unambiguously masculine: this, too, is part of the messenger's attraction for Olivia. Viola's tone is more akin to Feste's than to the laboured clichés of her would-be lover Orsino. Olivia's mock inventory of her looks may suggest an almost skittish, girlish joking, or it may be a more brittle self-mockery. This is a vulnerable person, hiding, perhaps, behind mourning and its physical symbol, the veil, here newly revealed. Her strange visitor is quick to characterise her, and not entirely flatteringly, describing Olivia as 'too proud', but with an apparently sincere tone, 'if you were the devil, you are fair' (lines 239–40). The 'text' has been left far behind, and this unscripted exchange turns up the heat in an already tense and expectant situation. There is a palpable energy in the conversation between the two women, as Viola finds herself the go-between and third party in an erotic triangle.

TEXT 2   VIOLA AND ORSINO DISCUSS MEN'S AND WOMEN'S LOVE (II.4.86–123)

VIOLA: But if she cannot love you, sir?

ORSINO: It cannot be so answered.

VIOLA: Sooth, but you must.
Say that some lady, as perhaps there is,
Hath for your love as great a pang of heart
As you have for Olivia. You cannot love her.   90
You tell her so. Must she not then be answered?

ORSINO: There is no woman's sides
Can bide the beating of so strong a passion
As love doth give my heart; no woman's heart
So big to hold so much; they lack retention.   95
Alas, their love may be called appetite,
No motion of the liver, but the palate,
That suffer surfeit, cloyment, and revolt.
But mine is all as hungry as the sea,
And can digest as much. Make no compare   100
Between that love a woman can bear me
And that I owe Olivia.

VIOLA: Ay, but I know –

ORSINO: What dost thou know?

VIOLA: Too well what love women to men may owe.
In faith, they are as true of heart as we.   105
My father had a daughter loved a man –
As it might be perhaps, were I a woman,
I should your lordship.

ORSINO: And what's her history?

VIOLA: A blank, my lord. She never told her love,
But let concealment, like a worm i' the bud,   110
Feed on her damask cheek. She pined in thought,
And with a green and yellow melancholy,
She sat like Patience on a monument,
Smiling at grief. Was not this love indeed?
We men may say more, swear more, but indeed   115
Our shows are more than will; for still we prove
Much in our vows, but little in our love.

ORSINO: But died thy sister of her love, my boy?

VIOLA: I am all the daughters of my father's house,
And all the brothers too; and yet I know not ...   120
Sir, shall I to this lady?

ORSINO: Ay, that's the theme.
To her in haste; give her this jewel; say,
My love can give no place, bide no denay.

Viola's attempts to persuade Orsino that Olivia may not love him employ
a kind of reverse psychology: she does not agree with him that women
are incapable of 'so strong a passion' (line 93) but rather tries to make
him believe that women bear a more constant love than men. She tells
him how women's love can be as strong as men's by encouraging him
to imagine that a woman loves him as much as he loves Olivia. It
is the first of the manoeuvres by which this oblique, yet intimate,
conversation progresses. Viola confesses her love for Orsino via imaginary
triangulations with this woman who might possibly love him, and
through her sister who loved but never articulated it.

Viola suggests that she might, were she a woman, love Orsino as
her sister (or with even more circumlocution, her father's daughter) loved

a man. Interestingly, she seems to dare to broach this only in the context of his rejection of her love: 'You cannot love her. / You tell her so' (lines 90–1). She counters Orsino's easy assumption that passionate love is an exclusively masculine quality with the image of the constant, pining woman who 'sat like Patience on a monument, / Smiling at grief' (lines 113–14). Orsino becomes interested in this tale, but his own masochistic interpretation of true love is displayed in his question 'But died thy sister of her love' (line 118). Perhaps the familiar address 'my boy' at the end of this line is the nearest Orsino gets to explicit affection for his page. The word 'love' breathes like a sigh through the lines as both characters nurse a love that cannot be requited. Viola's vacillation between her female self – 'I am all the daughters of my father's house' (line 119), and her male appearance – 'We men' (line 115), comes as close as she dares to revealing herself (see Themes, on Gender). Adopting the fake first person plural 'we' and the equally bogus third person 'she' shows how desperately Viola is thinking about different identities and the strain of these adjustments during her disguise. Almost her only use of the pronoun 'I' in the scene comes as a conditional: 'were I a woman' (line 107).

The **dramatic irony** of Orsino's glib sexism, 'man to man' with the woman whom he does not know is in love with him, makes for comedy as well as pathos in the scene. Orsino is almost competitive in the extent of his love, an appetite 'as hungry as the sea' (line 99) in an image which connects him to Viola, spat out by the sea on the shore of Illyria in I.2. In contrast to his imagery of love as ravenous eating (see Themes, on Excess), Viola's imaginary sister is eaten up by her unspoken love, 'like a worm i' the bud' (line 110) an image of something destroyed before it has the chance even to blossom. The imagery seems to suggest that it is Orsino's love which is active and masculine, and Viola's which is passive and feminine, but in fact neither is true: throughout, Viola has been a kind of catalyst or active agent (see Characterisation) and, as V.1 shows, Orsino reacts rather than instigates.

The account of the 'blank' history of Viola's father's daughter (line 109) is a shadow of how this play of unrequited love could, but won't, turn out. It is one of the ways the comedy flirts, albeit momentarily, with the 'what if' of tragedy. We already know that Sebastian is not drowned and can see that somehow matters will be resolved. But the scene ends in sadness and an abrupt change of mood. Viola recalls her brother (line 120) and stirs herself to go to Olivia on Orsino's suit. However, the closeness of this private conversation between Viola and Orsino contrasts with the distant formality of his wooing of Olivia, sending his page with a jewel rather than going in person. But this exchange with Viola has established the basis of their ultimate marriage, and we do not see Orsino again, because we do not need to, until the very last scene of the play.

TEXT 3 OLIVIA DECLARES HER LOVE FOR CESARIO (III.1.108–61)

OLIVIA: Give me leave, beseech you. I did send,
After the last enchantment you did here,
A ring in chase of you. So did I abuse   110
Myself, my servant, and, I fear me, you.
Under your hard construction must I sit,
To force that on you, in a shameful cunning
Which you knew none of yours. What might you think?
Have you not set mine honour at the stake,   115
And baited it with all th' unmuzzled thoughts
That tyrannous heart can think? To one of your receiving
Enough is shown; a cypress, not a bosom,
Hides my heart. So let me hear you speak.

VIOLA: I pity you.   120

OLIVIA: That's a degree to love.

VIOLA: No, not a grize; for 'tis a vulgar proof,
That very oft we pity enemies.

OLIVIA: Why, then, methinks 'tis time to smile again.
O world, how apt the poor are to be proud!
If one should be a prey, how much the better   125
To fall before the lion than the wolf!
                    Clock strikes
The clock upbraids me with the waste of time.
Be not afraid, good youth; I will not have you.

And yet, when wit and youth is come to harvest,
Your wife is like to reap a proper man.   130
There lies your way, due west.

VIOLA: Then westward ho!
Grace and good disposition attend your ladyship.
You'll nothing, madam, to my lord by me?

OLIVIA: Stay.
I prithee, tell me what thou think'st of me?   135

VIOLA: That you do think you are not what you are.

OLIVIA: If I think so, I think the same of you.

VIOLA: Then think you right; I am not what I am.

OLIVIA: I would you were as I would have you be.

VIOLA: Would it be better, madam, than I am? 140
I wish it might, for now I am your fool.

OLIVIA: (*aside*) O, what a deal of scorn looks beautiful
In the contempt and anger of his lip!
A murderous guilt shows not itself more soon
Than love that would seem hid; love's night is noon. 145
(*To* VIOLA) Cesario, by the roses of the spring,
By maidhood, honour, truth, and everything,
I love thee so that, maugre all thy pride,
Nor wit nor reason can my passion hide.
Do not extort thy reasons from this clause: 150
For that I woo, thou therefore hast no cause.
But rather reason thus with reason fetter:
Love sought, is good, but given unsought, is better.

VIOLA: By innocence I swear, and by my youth,
I have one heart, one bosom, and one truth. 155
And that no woman has, nor never none
Shall mistress be of it, save I alone.
And so, adieu, good madam; never more
Will I my master's tears to you deplore.

OLIVIA: Yet come again; for thou perhaps mayst move 160
That heart, which now abhors, to like his love.

When they last met, Viola called the shots and dominated the conversation (see Text 1). Here the tables are turned and it is Olivia who is setting the pace. Her first speech is full of condemnation of herself and, by implication, of Cesario for her previous behaviour in sending after him with a ring. Their earlier meeting is described as 'the last enchantment' (line 109). Olivia's sense of being entrapped by her sudden love for Orsino's messenger is conveyed in the image of herself as a bear 'at the stake' (line 115). Her speech is expressive of confused and passionate feeling, with **rhetorical** questions, a **hypermetric** line suggesting thoughts which cannot be contained by the regular **iambic pentameter** (line 117), heavy punctuation in the middle of lines giving a jerky feel to the flow of the verse. Olivia moves from blaming herself for her own 'shameful cunning' (line 113) to blaming Cesario for cruelly 'bait[ing]' her heart (line 116).

After this long outburst of pent-up and unaccustomed feeling, Viola's response is laconic: 'I pity you' (line 120). Olivia is so desperate that she seizes on this as positive evidence of Cesario's feelings for her, but Viola quickly disabuses her of that comfort: 'very oft we pity enemies' (line 122). Olivia responds with more animal imagery (line 116) in a speech of self-mockery. The intrusion of the clock breaks the intensity of the scene, or rather shifts it into a different key. Olivia's sudden awareness of 'the waste of time' (line 127) seems less about the immediate situation than a remark about her wider circumstances, committed to spending her own youth in long mourning. This realisation seems to cause her to relax her emotional grip on Cesario: 'I will not have you' (line 128), predicting instead some later marriage, but this is only a temporary relinquishing.

There is a desperation in Olivia's sudden, abrupt question: 'tell me what thou thinkst of me?', and this inaugurates a quick sequence of responses between the two in a **rhetorical** exchange known technically as **stichomythia**. But the sentences themselves are like a flourish of Feste's wit, prickling with syntactical and logical **paradoxes** about the gaps between seeming, being and knowing. Neither seems able to speak clearly: Olivia because of her heightened feelings, Viola because she cannot reveal her true self but can only allude to it in enigmatic formulae such as 'I am not what I am'.

Cesario does not, cannot return Olivia's strength of feeling, but there is a humorous aspect to Olivia's **aside** admiring his angry countenance: 'you're very sexy when you're angry'. This prompts an outright declaration: 'I love thee so' (line 148). She uses here the intimate 'thee' form. Viola cannot be equally frank in reply, although she tries to hint again at her real situation: 'no woman has, nor never none / Shall be mistress' of her heart, 'save I alone' (lines 156–7). The retreat into **rhyming couplets** which began with Olivia's avowal of love at line 146 seems to suggest a kind of deliberateness of expression, a desire not to be misunderstood, a formal, deep-breath kind of delivery. Yet Olivia will not take no for an answer, and is undeterred by the vehemence of Cesario's response. She invites him to continue his efforts to woo her for Orsino.

PART FIVE

Background

William Shakespeare

There are no personal records of Shakespeare's life. Official documents and occasional references to him by contemporaries enable us to draw the main outline of his public life, but his private life remains hidden. Although not at all unusual for a writer of his time, this lack of first-hand evidence has tempted many to read his plays as personal records and to look in them for clues to Shakespeare's own character and convictions. The results are unconvincing, partly because Renaissance art was not subjective or designed primarily to express the creator's personality, and partly because the drama of any period is very difficult to read biographically. Except when plays are written by committed dramatists to promote social or political causes (as by Shaw or Brecht), it is all but impossible to decide who amongst the variety of fictional characters in a drama represents the dramatist, or which of the various and often conflicting points of view expressed is authorial.

What we do know about Shakespeare's life can be quickly summarised. Shakespeare was born into a well-to-do family in the market town of Stratford-upon-Avon in Warwickshire in 1564, and was baptised in the town's Holy Trinity Church on 26 April. His father, John Shakespeare, was a prosperous glover (presumably this suggested the image Shakespeare gives to Feste of the sentence like 'a cheveril glove to a good wit; how quickly the wrong side may be turned outward' [III.1.12–13]) and leather merchant who became a person of some importance in the town: in 1565 he was elected an alderman and in 1568 he became high bailiff, or mayor of Stratford. He married Mary Arden in 1557, and William was the third of their eight children and their eldest son. It seems probable that William went to the local grammar school where he, like all Elizabethan schoolboys, would have studied a curriculum of Latin, history, logic and rhetoric. In November 1582, when he was aged eighteen, William married Anne Hathaway, who was twenty-six. The birth of their first daughter, Susanna, six months later in May 1983, suggests either that the couple married in haste when they learned of Anne's pregnancy or that there was some kind of civil contract before the marriage ceremony. Twins, Hamnet and Judith, were born to the marriage in 1585, so Shakespeare had direct experience of this phenomenon. He must, therefore, have known that non-identical twins rarely look so alike as to be mistaken for each other. Hamnet died in 1596: notwithstanding the difficulty of biographical readings of the plays, perhaps *Twelfth Night* provided Shakespeare with a fictive opportunity to reunite separated siblings and to bring a male twin back from apparent death.

The first time we hear of Shakespeare in London is in 1592 when he is mentioned as an actor and playwright by the dramatist Robert Greene. These 'lost years' 1585–92 have been the subject of much speculation, but how they were occupied remains as much of a mystery as when Shakespeare left Stratford and why. In his pamphlet, *Greene's Groatsworth of Wit*, Greene expresses to his fellow dramatists his outrage that the 'upstart crow' Shakespeare has the impudence to believe he 'is as well able to bombast out a blank verse as the best of you'. To have aroused this hostility from a rival, Shakespeare must, by 1592, have been long enough in London to have made a name for himself as a playwright. We may conjecture that he had left Stratford in 1586 or 1587.

During the next twenty years, Shakespeare continued to live in London, presumably visiting his wife and family in Stratford. He continued to act, but his chief fame was as a dramatist. From 1594 he wrote exclusively for the Lord Chamberlain's Men which rapidly became the leading dramatic company and from 1603 enjoyed the patronage of James I as the King's Men. His plays were popular and he became a shareholder in the profitable theatre company, earning enough money to buy land and a large house in Stratford. He retired to his home town in about 1611, and died there on 23 April 1616. He was buried in Holy Trinity Church.

His dramatic career

Between the late 1580s and 1613 Shakespeare wrote thirty-seven plays, and contributed to some by other dramatists. This was by no means an exceptional number for a professional playwright of the times, particularly in the context of a theatre industry which was hungry for new plays, each of which would probably have fewer than ten performances. The exact date of the composition of individual plays is a matter of debate – for only a few plays is the date of their first performance known – but the broad outlines of Shakespeare's dramatic career have been established. He began in the late 1580s and early 1590s with comedies, such as *The Comedy of Errors* which was heavily dependent on its source, the Latin playwright Plautus, with plays based on English history and the Wars of the Roses (*Henry VI* parts 1, 2 and 3, and *Richard III*), and with the bloodthirsty revenge tragedy *Titus Andronicus*. During the 1590s Shakespeare developed his expertise in comedies, writing plays such as *A Midsummer Night's Dream* and *As You Like It*, and produced further plays on medieval English history including *Henry IV* and *Henry V*. *Twelfth Night* is usually dated at the end of this period.

As the new century begins a new note is detectable. Plays such as *Troilus and Cressida* (1601–2) and *Measure for Measure*, sometimes designated 'problem plays' as they poise between comedy and tragedy, evoke complex responses. These plays offer a chronological and generic bridge between the comic period of the 1590s and Shakespeare's tragedies, including *Othello*, *King Lear*, *Macbeth*, *Coriolanus* and *Antony and Cleopatra*, all written in the first decade of the seventeenth century. In the last years of his dramatic career, Shakespeare produced a group of plays often called 'romances'. These plays – *The Tempest*, *Cymbeline* and *The Winter's Tale* – reprise many of the situations and themes of the earlier dramas but in fantastical and exotic dramatic designs which, set in distant lands, covering large tracts of time and involving music, mime, dance and tableaux, have something of the qualities of masques and pageants.

THE TEXTS OF SHAKESPEARE'S PLAYS

None of Shakespeare's plays exists in the author's manuscript. Nineteen were printed (but not *Twelfth Night*) during his lifetime in small, cheap books called quartos. Shakespeare, however, did not supervise the publication of these plays. This was not unusual. When a playwright had sold a play to a dramatic company he sold his rights in it: copyright, in as much as it existed at this time, belonged to whoever had possession of an actual copy of the text, and so consequently authors had no control over what happened to their work. Several of the quartos do not even mention Shakespeare's name on their title-pages. Unlike the case of a modern author who would prepare his or her work carefully for publication and would receive proof-copies to check for printing errors before the work was circulated, Elizabethan and Jacobean dramatic texts find their way into print in various non-authorial ways. Sometimes an actor's copy of the script, or a prompt copy, perhaps cut or altered for performance, was the basis of the printed text; other quartos seem to derive from an actor or audience member's memory of the play. Printers introduced their own errors, through misreading or making their own 'corrections' where they considered it necessary. Some play-texts, for example the earliest publication of Shakespeare's *Richard II*, also show the marks of censorship.

In 1623, seven years after Shakespeare's death, John Heminges and Henry Condell, two of his fellow actors, collected together texts of thirty-six of his plays (*Pericles* was omitted) and published them together in a large book known as the First Folio. There were later editions in 1632, 1663 and 1685. Heminges and Condell promised their readers that these were the texts as Shakespeare had intended them, but this may have been a marketing ploy rather like those modern films which are remarketed as 'the director's cut' despite being essentially the same product as was already available. Despite its appearance and their assurances of its authority, however, the texts in the First Folio still present many difficulties, for there are printing errors and confused passages in the plays, and its texts often differ significantly from those of the earlier quartos, when these exist.

In the case of the text of *Twelfth Night*, the play was first published in the First Folio. There are a number of passages and phrases, known as **cruces**, which have been the subject of intense labour by bibliographers, textual critics and editors. Most modern editions give an abbreviated account of the Folio text (sometimes denoted simply as F) alongside their modernised and emended version, either as a section of collation between the text and the explanatory notes (as in the Arden and World's Classics editions) or as an appendix (as in the Penguin edition). So, for example, the Penguin editor M.M. Mahood lists over forty minor alterations she has made to the Folio text, such as 'leman' (meaning lover) for the Folio's 'lemon' (II.3.24). Her substitution of 'dun-coloured' for the Folio's 'damn'd colour'd' (I.3.128) is one possible emendation: the Oxford edition, edited by Stanley Wells and Roger Warren gives 'divers-coloured', and 'lemon-coloured' (attractive, given Olivia's dislike of yellow) and 'flame-coloured' have also been proposed. Modern editions also include numerous additional stage directions, which are often very sparse in early texts.

Shakespeare's texts have, then, been through a number of intermediaries, both in his period and in our own. We do not have his authority for any one of his plays, and hence we cannot know exactly what it was that he wrote. Bibliographers, textual critics and editors have spent a great deal of effort on endeavouring to get behind the apparent errors, uncertainties and contradictions in the available texts to recover the plays as Shakespeare originally wrote them. What we read is the result of these efforts. Modern texts are what editors have constructed from the available evidence: they correspond to no sixteenth- or seventeenth-century editions, and to no early performance of a Shakespeare play. Furthermore, these composite texts differ from each other, for different editors read the early texts differently, perceive different problems, and then come to different conclusions. A Shakespeare text is an unstable and a contrived thing.

Often, of course, its judgements embody, if not the personal prejudices of the editor, then the cultural preferences of the time in which he or she was working, Growing awareness of this has led recent scholars to distrust the whole editorial enterprise, and to repudiate the attempt to construct a 'perfect' text. Stanley Wells and Gary Taylor, the editors of the Oxford edition of *The Complete Works* (1986), point out that almost certainly the texts of Shakespeare's plays were altered in performance, and from one performance to another, so that there may never have been a single version. They note, too, that Shakespeare probably revised and rewrote some plays. They do not claim to print a definitive text of any play, but prefer what seems to them the 'more theatrical' version, and when there is a great difference between available versions, as with *King Lear*, they print two texts.

Shakespeare arrived in London at the very time that the Elizabethan period was poised to become the 'golden age' of English Literature. Although Elizabeth reigned as queen from 1558 to 1603, the term 'Elizabethan' is used very loosely in a literary sense to refer to the period 1580 to 1625 when the great works of the age were produced. (Sometimes the later part of this period is distinguished as 'Jacobean', from the Latin form of the name of Elizabeth's successor, James VI of Scotland and I of England, who reigned from 1603 to 1625.) The poet Edmund Spenser heralded this new literary age with his pastoral poem *The Shepheardes Calender* (1579), and in his essay *An Apologie for Poetrie* (written in about 1580 and published in 1595), his patron Sir Philip Sidney championed the imaginative power of the 'speaking picture of poetry', famously declaring that 'Nature never set forth the earth in so rich a tapestry as divers poets have done ... Her world is brazen, the poets only deliver a golden'.

Spenser and Sidney were part of that rejuvenating movement in European culture which since the nineteenth century has been known by the term *Renaissance*. Meaning literally 'rebirth' it denotes a revival and redirection of artistic and intellectual endeavour which began in Italy in the fourteenth century and reached England in the early sixteenth century. Its keynote was a curiosity in thought which challenged the old assumptions and traditions: as the poet John Donne was to put it in 'An Anatomy of the World' published in 1633, 'new Philosophy calls all in doubt'. To the innovative spirit of the Renaissance, the preceding ages appeared dully unoriginal and conformist, what the critic C.S. Lewis has termed 'the drab age'.

That spirit was fuelled by the rediscovery of many classical texts and the culture of ancient Greece and Rome. This fostered a confidence in human reason and in human potential which, in every sphere, challenged old convictions. The discovery of America and its peoples (Columbus had sailed in 1492) demonstrated that the world was a larger and stranger place than had been thought. The cosmological speculation of Copernicus (later confirmed by Galileo) that the sun, not the earth, was the centre of the planetary system challenged the centuries-old belief that the earth and human beings were at the centre of the universe. The pragmatic political philosophy of Machiavelli seemed to cut politics free from its traditional link with morality, by advising statesmen to use any means to secure a desired end. And the religious movements we know collectively as the Reformation broke with the Roman Catholic church and set the individual conscience, not ecclesiastical authority, at the centre of religious life. Nothing, it seemed, was beyond questioning, nothing impossible, although the fate of the hero of Marlowe's play *Dr Faustus* showed the limits and dangers of such radical freedom. The term 'Renaissance' suggests that this age defined itself in relation to the past. Some historians and literary scholars have preferred to use a term which stresses the period's relationship to the future: 'early modern'. Whereas the idea of the Renaissance focuses intellectual and artistic developments, the early modern period stresses those features of life more familiar to us now – with changing ideas of society, of family, of sexuality and the roles of men and women, with the operations of class or rank, with urban life, economics and questions of personal and cultural identity.

Shakespeare's drama is a product of its age, as well as of its creator, in its innovative and challenging stance. It interrogates (examines and asks questions of) the beliefs, assumptions and politics upon which Elizabethan society was founded. And although the plays often conclude in a restoration of order and stability, many critics are inclined to argue that their imaginative energy goes into subverting, rather than reinforcing, traditional values such as, for example, gender in *Twelfth Night*.

Shakespeare's theatre

The theatre for which Shakespeare wrote his plays was a distinctly Elizabethan invention. There had been no theatres or acting companies during the medieval period, when plays – usually on religious subjects – were performed by travelling groups of players in market-places, inn yards and in the halls of great houses. Such actors were regarded by the authorities as little better than vagabonds and layabouts.

In the late sixteenth century, circumstances coincided to transform this situation. One influence was intellectual. A number of young men who had been to the universities of Oxford and Cambridge came to London in the 1580s and began to write plays based on their knowledge of classical dramas of ancient Greece and Rome. John Lyly, Christopher

Marlowe and Thomas Kyd wrote full-length plays on secular subjects, offering a range of characterisation and situation hitherto unattempted in English drama. Lyly wrote in prose, but the other playwrights composed in the unrhymed **iambic pentameters** (blank verse) which the Earl of Surrey had introduced into English earlier in the sixteenth century. This was a freer and more expressive medium than the rhymed verse of medieval drama.

Another influence on the establishment of a professional theatre was a new law forbidding travelling players unless they were under the patronage of a nobleman. (Shakespeare's company was under the patronage of the Lord Chamberlain.) This ensured that only the best troupes survived, and that their activity centred on London, where their patrons attended the queen at her court. In 1576 the entrepreneur James Burbage built the first permanent playhouse, called 'The Theatre' in Shoreditch just beyond London's northern boundary. Other theatre buildings followed, mostly just outside the city walls or on the south bank of the river Thames to avoid the regulations of London's civic authorities. The design of these playhouses was based on that of bear-baiting arenas, and the theatre continued to be associated with this popular bloodsport. The theatre was not the respectable middle-class institution of modern times: it was identified with prostitution, pickpocketing and with the spread of plague. It was blamed for encouraging idleness and criminality, and some extreme preachers argued that the whole system of acting was a form of lying and therefore of sin. Local residents complained about the numbers of people who congregated at the theatre, and, when carriages became popular in the Jacobean period, the congestion on London Bridge caused by playgoers prompted the first parking regulations.

Shakespeare's company performed at Burbage's Theatre until 1596, and also used the Swan and Curtain theatres until moving into their own new building, the Globe, in 1599. It was burned down in 1613 when the thatched roof was ignited by a spark from a cannon fired during a performance of Shakespeare's *Henry VIII*. The Globe theatre has recently been reconstructed, using the available evidence, on Bankside, which offers some sense of the experience of theatregoing for Shakespeare's audiences.

THE GLOBE THEATRE.

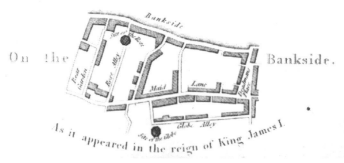

On the Bankside.

As it appeared in the reign of King James I.

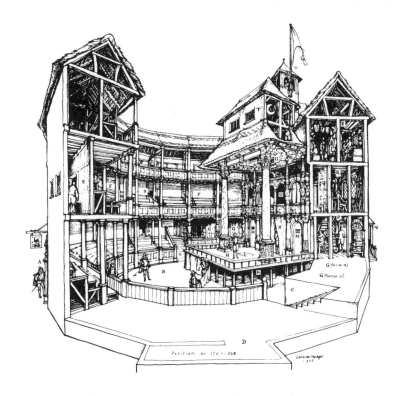

A CONJECTURAL RECONSTRUCTION OF THE INTERIOR OF THE GLOBE PLAYHOUSE

AA Main entrance
B   The Yard
CC Entrances to lowest galleries
D   Entrance to staircase and upper galleries
E   Corridor serving the different sections of the middle gallery
F   Middle gallery ('Twopenny Rooms')
G   'Gentlemen's Rooms or Lords Rooms'
H   The stage
J   The hanging being put up round the stage
K   The 'Hell' under the stage
L   The stage trap, leading down to the Hell
MM Stage doors

N   Curtained 'place behind the stage'
O   Gallery above the stage, used as required sometimes by musicians, sometimes by spectators, and often as part of the play
P   Back-stage area (the tiring-house)
Q   Tiring-house door
R   Dressing-rooms
S   Wardrobe and storage
T   The hut housing the machine for lowering enthroned gods, etc., to the stage
U   The 'Heavens'
W   Hoisting the playhouse flag

The form of the Elizabethan theatre derived from the inn yards and animal baiting rings which provided other kinds of entertainment. They were circular wooden buildings with a paved courtyard in the middle open to the sky. A rectangular stage jutted out into the yard, or pit, where some audience members paid a penny to stand and watch the play. Round the perimeter of the yard were tiered galleries, covered with thatch, providing more expensive seats for wealthier spectators. Performances took place in the afternoons to make use of daylight. The yard was just over 24 metres in diameter, the stage measured 12 by 9 metres at 1.67 metres high, and the theatre could hold about 3,000 spectators. The stage itself was partially covered by a roof or canopy which projected from the wall at the rear of the stage and was supported by two posts at the front. Two doors at the back of the stage led into the dressing room (or 'tiring house') and it was by means of these doors that actors entered and left the stage. Between the doors was a small recess or alcove which was curtained off to provide a 'discovery space', and over the discovery space was a balcony. In the early years of the seventeenth century, Shakespeare's company acquired a smaller indoor theatre called Blackfriars which could seat about 700 people. As a more expensive venue, this theatre probably catered to an audience of a higher social rank. Blackfriars had facilities for more elaborate stage effects, including a machine for lowering actors from above the stage, and these new possibilities were incorporated in Shakespeare's late plays.

There was little in the way of large-scale scenery, which is why Shakespeare's characters often tell us at great length where they are or what their surroundings are like or that it is dark or dawn or stormy. As locations were not represented visually, they have more power as symbolic places, perhaps suggesting an inner landscape or psychological state rather than a specific geographical place. Props and costumes were probably also limited. All the roles, including women, were played by male actors. This is particularly significant for *Twelfth Night*: when Viola dresses in male clothes to become Cesario, the layers of pretence are multiplied as, of course, 'Viola' is played by a male actor in the first place. These factors, together with the form of the playhouse, meant that audiences were always aware that they were watching a play. The drama of the period often draws explicit attention to itself *as* drama, using nonnaturalistic conventions such as **soliloquy**, the imagery of theatrical performance, exploring issues of disguise, role-playing, and the gap between appearance and reality.

The early modern theatre was not concerned to make its audience believe what it was watching was really happening – the recognition of the artificiality of the spectacle was key to the theatrical experience. Modern theatres, by contrast, use lighting and conventions of audience behaviour to encourage spectators to forget themselves as they become absorbed by the action on stage. The auditorium is usually dark, with a passive, silent and attentive audience watching a spotlit stage where actors are vocal, demonstrative and dramatic. By all accounts, Shakespeare's theatre was quite different. Audience members went to be seen as much as to see, they were lit by natural light like the actors and wore the same kind of clothing. They had none of our modern deference, arriving late, talking and heckling during the performance, eating, drinking and conducting business. It was all much more like our experience of pantomime, where the artificiality of its conventions are enjoyed, expected and understood. But calling a theatre 'the Globe' suggests that it is a microcosm of the world, and the theatre did provide Elizabethan culture with a **metaphor** for understanding its own existence, as in Shakespeare's own famous observation 'All the world's a stage' (*As You Like It*). This philosophy is elaborated in this short poem by Sir Walter Raleigh:

> What is our life? The play of passion.
> Our mirth? The music of division:
> Our mothers' wombs the tiring-houses be,
> Where we are dressed for life's short comedy.
> The earth the stage; Heaven the spectator is,
> Who sits and views whosoe'er doth act amiss.
> The graves which hide us from the scorching sun
> Are like drawn curtains when the play is done.
> Thus playing post we to our latest rest,
> And then we die in earnest, not in jest.

SOURCES

Shakespeare hardly ever invented his own plots – attitudes to literary originality were rather different in the Elizabethan period from our own views – preferring to take episodes and narratives from existing stories, often translations from European languages. His method in writing *Twelfth Night* was no different. The ultimate source for the play is an Italian drama called *Gl'Ingannati* (The Deceived Ones), performed in Siena in 1531 and reprinted numerous times during the century. We do not know, however, whether Shakespeare had access to this text in its original form. It is more likely that he knew of it at second, or even third hand, via Barnabe Riche's prose tale of Apolonius and Silla, part of his *Riche his Farewell to Militarie Profession* (1581). Riche's story, in outline, is of Apolonius, a young Duke visiting Cyprus where the daughter of his host, Silla, falls in love with him but cannot get him to notice her. Apolonius leaves Cyprus for his home, Silla follows him by boat but is the only survivor of a shipwreck. She disguises herself as a man, assumes the name of her brother, Silvio, currently serving as a soldier in Africa, and gets herself a position at Apolonius's court. Apolonius is courting a wealthy widow, Julina, and sends Silla as his messenger. Julina falls in love with Silla. When the real Silvio arrives to search for his sister, Julina mistakes him for the Duke's messenger and spends the night with him, conceiving a child as a result. Silvio leaves the city, and Julina claims Silla as the father. Silla is so amazed at this claim that she confesses her real identity to Julina, who tells Apolonius, who is so impressed by Silla's devotion to him that he marries her. The real Silvio hears of the situation, and stricken with remorse about Julina, marries her. All lived happily ever after.

Shakespeare's main adaptation of the story is to simplify it – Viola does not already know Orsino, as Silla does Apolonius – and to romanticise it – Olivia falls quickly in love with Sebastian and their marriage is indeed hasty, but it precedes a sexual encounter between them. Shakespeare also makes use of his own play *Comedy of Errors*, as John Manningham noticed (see Note on the Text). In this play, confusion over the identities of twins predominates, including the mistaken request for money from the wrong twin, as Antonio asks Viola in III.4.

PART SIX

CRITICAL HISTORY & BROADER PERSPECTIVES

EARLY CRITICS

Early critics of *Twelfth Night*, following John Manningham, took particular note of the Malvolio plot and a play entitled 'Malvolio' was performed in the seventeenth century. Samuel Johnson considered the steward 'truly comic', but criticised the play for its lack of 'credibility' in the matter of Olivia's marriage to Sebastian. For William Hazlitt, the play represented the 'ludicrous', making 'us laugh at the follies of mankind, not despise them, and still less bear any ill-will towards them', and he confessed to a sneaking 'regard for Malvolio'. Johnson and Hazlitt's critiques are included in D.J. Palmer's Casebook on the play (Macmillan, 1972). Other early nineteenth-century views are reprinted in Jonathan Bate's collection *The Romantics on Shakespeare* (Penguin, 1992), including the German critic August Schlegel's observation that the play 'unites the entertainment of an intrigue, contrived with great ingenuity, to a rich fund of comic characters and situations and the beauteous colours of ethereal poetry'. Charles Lamb, like Hazlitt, values Malvolio, arguing that 'even in his abused state of chains and darkness, a sort of greatness seems never to desert him', and concluding that the 'catastrophe of this character [has] a kind of tragic interest'.

APPROACHES TO THE PLAY

Three basic movements in the history of the literary reception of comedies can be traced. Up until the middle of the twentieth century, comedies were seen as escapist crowd-pleasers, whose unreality was part of their sentimental charm. This critical movement has its clearest expression in the title of John Dover Wilson's book of 1962, *Shakespeare's Happy Comedies* (Faber & Faber). Leslie Hotson's influential but ultimately unproven speculation that the play was written for performance at court on 6 January 1600 is also characteristic of this approach. Hotson's opening to his *The First Night of Twelfth Night*

(Rupert Hart-Davis, 1954) asks merrily, 'Is there anywhere a more delightful comedy than *Twelfth Night*? The cheerful gale of popular favour has sent it down the centuries full-sailed, on a sea of music and laughter.'

Around the 1950s, critics schooled in anthropological approaches to literature began to examine the comedies in the context of social myths and rituals, particularly important to *Twelfth Night*. C.L. Barber's influential book *Shakespeare's Festive Comedy* (Princeton University Press, 1959) relates Elizabethan drama to social customs and holiday comedy, and the chapter on the play identifies its power 'to move audiences through release to clarification, making distinctions between false care and true freedom'.

By contrast, most recent criticism has been concerned with the comedies as unresolved and problematic – in social, linguistic, gender or psychoanalytic terms. Different critics' interpretations of the ending of the play give a good idea of where they stand. The first two movements are represented in D.J. Palmer's collection of essays and critical extracts in the Casebook series volume on *Twelfth Night* (1972). In this collection, C.L. Barber argues that the reversal of sexual roles in the play consolidates rather than threatens the *status quo* and John Russell Brown suggests some questions for performance such as the nature of Illyria, the play's time-scheme, and its characterisation. Ultimately Palmer's selection of critics endorses an idea of the play's unity and ultimate resolution.

The third aspect of criticism is exemplified in the New Casebook volume, edited by R.S. White (Macmillan, 1996). Here, Geoffrey Hartman argues that the play is so preoccupied by **puns** and witty **rhetoric** that it is language in its slipperiness and vitality that becomes its central theme. In contrast to C.L. Barber, Michael Bristol suggests that the relationship between **carnival** and theatre permanently challenges, rather than endorses, social order. The play's different and complex depictions of gender and sexuality are discussed in essays by Stephen Greenblatt and Dympna Callaghan. Callaghan challenges the heterosexual assumptions of critics who stress the play's ultimate marriage resolutions while suppressing the troubling desire of Orsino for his page, Olivia for a woman, and Antonio for his young master, and reminds us of the significance of the fact that these plays were originally performed by all-male casts. Whereas the essays in the earlier volume stress unity of theme and construction, these later pieces pick out discordant or dissonant elements to stress the play's darker and more problematic aspects.

The play's representation of gender and sexuality has been one of the most fruitful areas for recent scholarship. In a chapter in his book *Impersonations: the Performance of Gender in Shakespeare's England* (Cambridge University Press, 1996), Stephen Orgel stresses the complications of the fact that Viola's part would have originally been played by a male actor. He also examines why Viola opts to disguise herself as a 'eunuch', or castrated male, rather than as a young or immature man. The play's homoerotic potential is discussed by Valerie Traub in her *Desire and Anxiety: Circulations of Sexuality in Shakespearean Drama* (Routledge, 1992), and by Joseph Pequigney in 'The Two Antonios and Same Sex Love in *The Merchant of Venice* and *Twelfth Night*'. Pequigney discusses the two plays' Antonio characters, both of whom are identified in passionate, self-sacrificial relation to other men and both of whom are left unmarried and unresolved at the end of their respective play. The essay is reprinted in Deborah Barker and Ivo Kamps's collection, *Shakespeare and Gender: A History* (Verso, 1995). In her book *Still Harping on Daughters: Women and Drama in the Age of Shakespeare* (Columbia University Press, second edition 1989), Lisa Jardine argues that men playing women's roles is a performance intended to titillate a male audience, and she quotes extensively from contemporary anti-theatrical pamphlets to support this proposition.

Twelfth Night has been a popular play in the theatre, and information from theatre practitioners about the play is an extremely useful aspect of its critical history. Zoë Wanamaker discusses her role as Viola in *Players of Shakespeare 2* edited by Russell Jackson and Robert Smallwood (Cambridge University Press, 1988), and Michael Pennington draws on his experience of directing the play for his detailed *Twelfth Night: A User's Guide* (Nick Hern Books, 2000). Michael Billington talks to directors in his *Directors' Shakespeare: Approaches to Twelfth Night* (Nick Hern Books, 1990) and Lois Potter considers four productions of the play in *Twelfth Night: Text and Performance* (Macmillan, 1985).

Finally, the most accessible recent discussion of Shakespeare's comedies is Michael Mangan's highly recommended *A Preface to Shakespeare's Comedies 1594–1603* (Longman, 1996). Mangan discusses comedy as structure and as humour, with reference to the contemporary context of the plays' performance, and then offers a series of detailed and stimulating readings of specific plays, including *Twelfth Night*.

World events	Author's life	Literary events
		1513 Niccolò Machiavelli, *The Prince*
		1528 Castiglione, *Book of the Courtier*
		1531 *Gl'Ingannati* (source)
1534 Henry VIII breaks with Rome		
1556 Archbishop Cranmer burnt at stake		
1558 Elizabeth I accedes to throne		
		1562 Lope de Vega, great Spanish dramatist, born
	1564 (26 April) William Shakespeare baptised, Stratford-upon-Avon	
1570 Elizabeth I excommunicated		
	1576 James Burbage builds the first theatre in England, at Shoreditch	
1577 Francis Drake sets out on voyage round the world		
		1580 (c) Sir Philip Sidney, *An Apologie for Poetrie*
		1581 *Riche his Farewell to Militarie Profession* (source)
	1582 Shakespeare marries Anne Hathaway	
	1583 Their daughter, Susanna, is born	
1584 Raleigh's sailors land in Virginia		
	1585 Their twins, Hamnet & Judith, born	
1587 Execution of Mary Queen of Scots		
1588 The Spanish Armada defeated		**1588-9** Thomas Kyd, *The Spanish Tragedy*
	late 1580s - early 90s Probably writes *Henry VI (Parts I, II, III)* and *Richard III*	**1590** Edmund Spenser, *Faerie Queene* (Books I-III)
1592 Plague in London closes theatres	**1592** Recorded as being a London actor and an 'upstart crow'	
	1592-4 Writes *Comedy of Errors*	
	1594 onwards Writes exclusively for the Lord Chamberlain's Men	

World events	Author's life	Literary events
	1595 (pre-) *Two Gentlemen of Verona, The Taming of the Shrew* and *Love's Labour's Lost* probably written	1595 Death of William Painter, whose *Palace of Pleasure* provided sources for plots of many Elizabethan dramas
	1595 (c) *Romeo and Juliet*	
1596 English raid on Cadiz	1596-8 Death of twin son, Hamnet; first performance, *The Merchant of Venice*	
	1598-9 Globe Theatre built at Southwark	
	1600 *A Midsummer Night's Dream, Much Ado about Nothing* and *The Merchant of Venice* printed in quartos	
	1600-1 *Hamlet*	
	1600-2 **Twelfth Night** written	
1603 Death of Queen Elizabeth Tudor; accession of James Stuart	1603 onwards His company enjoys patronage of James I as the King's Men	
	1604 *Othello* performed	
1605 Discovery of Guy Fawkes's plot	1605 First version of *King Lear*	1605 Cervantes, *Don Quijote de la Mancha*
	1606 *Macbeth*	
	1606-7 *Antony and Cleopatra*	
	1608 The King's Men acquire Blackfriars Theatre for winter performances	
1610 William Harvey discovers circulation of blood		
	1611 *Cymbeline, The Winter's Tale* and *The Tempest* performed	
1612 Last burning of heretics in England		
	1613 Globe Theatre burns down	
	1616 Death of William Shakespeare	
1618 Raleigh executed for treason Thirty Years War begins in Europe		
	1623 First folio of Shakespeare's works	

apostrophe a rhetorical term for a speech addressed to a person or thing

aside dramatic convention by which a character on stage says something that the audience can hear but not all the other characters

bathos, bathetic a ludicrous descent from the elevated treatment of a subject to the ordinary and dull

blank verse unrhymed lines of iambic pentameter

blazon a poetic device in which the lover's eyes, lips, cheeks and hair are catalogued and separately described

carnival a literary phenomenon described by the Russian critic Mikhail Bakhtin, especially in his work *Rabelais and his World* (1965). According to him some writers use their works as an outlet for the spirit of carnival, of popular festivity and *misrule*. They 'subvert' the literary culture of the ruling classes, undermining its claim to moral monopoly. Such forms and genres are open and 'dialogic'. They allow multiple points of view to co-exist and are valued for their availability to 'plural' interpretations

chorus, choric ancient Greek drama had a chorus, who usually acted as commentator rather than participant in the events, often with ironic insight

crux (pl., **cruces**) a difficult point in a text about which different critics and editors disagree

dramatic irony occurs when the development of the plot means that the audience is in possession of more information about what is happening than some of the characters are

etymology the study of the history and origins of words

eulogy formal speech of high praise or commendation

homophone a word which sounds identical to another but is spelt differently and has a different meaning (for example so/sew)

hyperbole a figure of speech: emphasis by exaggeration

hypermetric a line of verse with more syllables than its pattern (for example iambic pentameter) allows

iambic pentameter a line with five stressed beats, in a *ti-tum* weak-stress/strong-stress pattern

irony saying one thing while meaning another

metaphor, metaphorical a comparison of two things or ideas, which goes further than a simile, by fusing them together

Method technique of acting based on the theories of Russian actor and director Konstantin Stanislavsky (1863–1938) in which ideas about the inner motivations and psychology of a character are the basis of the performance

nonce word a word coined for a particular occasion

paradox, paradoxical an apparently self-contradictory statement with an underlying meaning or truth beneath its superficial absurdity

pentameter see iambic pentameter

Petrarch fourteenth-century Italian poet who wrote sonnets. **Petrarchan** suggests idealised, courtly and unrequited love, and the prominent use of paradoxes such as 'icy heat'

pun play on words, where two or more different meanings are drawn out of a single word for witty or comic effect

rhetoric the art of speaking (and writing) effectively so as to persuade an audience. Also used pejoratively to mean empty, bombastic prose

rhyming couplet a pair of rhymed lines

satire literature which examines vice and folly and makes them appear contemptible and ridiculous

soliloquy literally 'to speak alone' – hence a speech from a character when alone on stage, traditionally enabling him or her to express inner thoughts and feelings

sonnet lyric poem consisting of fourteen rhyming lines

stichomythia interchange of single lines in a dialogue, giving the impression of rapid but controlled arguments

verisimilitude likeness to reality

AUTHOR OF THIS NOTE

Emma Smith is a Fellow in English at Hertford College, Oxford. She is author of the Advanced York Note on *Measure for Measure*.

York Notes Advanced (£3.99 each)

Margaret Atwood
Cat's Eye

Margaret Atwood
The Handmaid's Tale

Jane Austen
Mansfield Park

Jane Austen
Persuasion

Jane Austen
Pride and Prejudice

Jane Austen
Sense and Sensibility

Alan Bennett
Talking Heads

William Blake
Songs of Innocence and of Experience

Charlotte Brontë
Jane Eyre

Charlotte Brontë
Villette

Emily Brontë
Wuthering Heights

Angela Carter
Nights at the Circus

Geoffrey Chaucer
The Franklin's Prologue and Tale

Geoffrey Chaucer
The Miller's Prologue and Tale

Geoffrey Chaucer
Prologue To the Canterbury Tales

Geoffrey Chaucer
The Wife of Bath's Prologue and Tale

Samuel Taylor Coleridge
Selected Poems

Joseph Conrad
Heart of Darkness

Daniel Defoe
Moll Flanders

Charles Dickens
Great Expectations

Charles Dickens
Hard Times

Emily Dickinson
Selected Poems

John Donne
Selected Poems

Carol Ann Duffy
Selected Poems

George Eliot
Middlemarch

George Eliot
The Mill on the Floss

T.S. Eliot
Selected Poems

F. Scott Fitzgerald
The Great Gatsby

E.M. Forster
A Passage to India

Brian Friel
Translations

Thomas Hardy
Jude the Obscure

Thomas Hardy
The Mayor of Casterbridge

Thomas Hardy
The Return of the Native

Thomas Hardy
Selected Poems

Thomas Hardy
Tess of the d'Urbervilles

Seamus Heaney
Selected Poems from Opened Ground

Nathaniel Hawthorne
The Scarlet Letter

Homer
The Odyssey

Kazuo Ishiguro
The Remains of the Day

Ben Jonson
The Alchemist

James Joyce
Dubliners

John Keats
Selected Poems

Christopher Marlowe
Doctor Faustus

Arthur Miller
Death of a Salesman

John Milton
Paradise Lost Books I & II

Toni Morrison
Beloved

Sylvia Plath
Selected Poems

Alexander Pope
Rape of the Lock and other poems

William Shakespeare
Antony and Cleopatra

William Shakespeare
As You Like It

William Shakespeare
Hamlet

William Shakespeare
King Lear

William Shakespeare
Macbeth

William Shakespeare
Measure for Measure

William Shakespeare
The Merchant of Venice

William Shakespeare
A Midsummer Night's Dream

William Shakespeare
Much Ado About Nothing

William Shakespeare
Othello

William Shakespeare
Richard II

William Shakespeare
Romeo and Juliet

William Shakespeare
The Taming of the Shrew

William Shakespeare
The Tempest

William Shakespeare
Twelfth Night

William Shakespeare
The Winter's Tale

George Bernard Shaw
Saint Joan

Mary Shelley
Frankenstein

Jonathan Swift
Gulliver's Travels and A Modest Proposal

Alfred, Lord Tennyson
Selected Poems

Alice Walker
The Color Purple

Oscar Wilde
The Importance of Being Earnest

Tennessee Williams
A Streetcar Named Desire

John Webster
The Duchess of Malfi

Virginia Woolf
To the Lighthouse

W.B. Yeats
Selected Poems

Jane Austen
Emma

Louis de Bernières
Captain Corelli's Mandolin

Caryl Churchill
Top Girls and *Cloud Nine*

Charles Dickens
Bleak House

T.S. Eliot
The Waste Land

Homer
The Iliad

Aldous Huxley
Brave New World

Christopher Marlowe
Edward II

George Orwell
Nineteen Eighty-four

William Shakespeare
Henry IV Pt I

William Shakespeare
Henry IV Part II

William Shakespeare
Richard III

Tom Stoppard
Arcadia and *Rosencrantz and Guildenstern are Dead*

Virgil
The Aeneid

Jeanette Winterson
Oranges are Not the Only Fruit

Tennessee Williams
Cat on a Hot Tin Roof

Metaphysical Poets

OTHER TITLES

GCSE and equivalent levels (£3.50 each)

Maya Angelou
I Know Why the Caged Bird Sings

Jane Austen
Pride and Prejudice

Alan Ayckbourn
Absent Friends

Elizabeth Barrett Browning
Selected Poems

Robert Bolt
A Man for All Seasons

Harold Brighouse
Hobson's Choice

Charlotte Brontë
Jane Eyre

Emily Brontë
Wuthering Heights

Shelagh Delaney
A Taste of Honey

Charles Dickens
David Copperfield

Charles Dickens
Great Expectations

Charles Dickens
Hard Times

Charles Dickens
Oliver Twist

Roddy Doyle
Paddy Clarke Ha Ha Ha

George Eliot
Silas Marner

George Eliot
The Mill on the Floss

Anne Frank
The Diary of Anne Frank

William Golding
Lord of the Flies

Oliver Goldsmith
She Stoops To Conquer

Willis Hall
The Long and the Short and the Tall

Thomas Hardy
Far from the Madding Crowd

Thomas Hardy
The Mayor of Casterbridge

Thomas Hardy
Tess of the d'Urbervilles

Thomas Hardy
The Withered Arm and other Wessex Tales

L.P. Hartley
The Go-Between

Seamus Heaney
Selected Poems

Susan Hill
I'm the King of the Castle

Barry Hines
A Kestrel for a Knave

Louise Lawrence
Children of the Dust

Harper Lee
To Kill a Mockingbird

Laurie Lee
Cider with Rosie

Arthur Miller
The Crucible

Arthur Miller
A View from the Bridge

Robert O'Brien
Z for Zachariah

Frank O'Connor
My Oedipus Complex and Other Stories

George Orwell
Animal Farm

J.B. Priestley
An Inspector Calls

J.B. Priestley
When We Are Married

Willy Russell
Educating Rita

Willy Russell
Our Day Out

J.D. Salinger
The Catcher in the Rye

William Shakespeare
Henry IV Part 1

William Shakespeare
Henry V

William Shakespeare
Julius Caesar

William Shakespeare
Macbeth

William Shakespeare
The Merchant of Venice

William Shakespeare
A Midsummer Night's Dream

William Shakespeare
Much Ado About Nothing

William Shakespeare
Romeo and Juliet

William Shakespeare
The Tempest

William Shakespeare
Twelfth Night

George Bernard Shaw
Pygmalion

Mary Shelley
Frankenstein

R.C. Sherriff
Journey's End

Rukshana Smith
Salt on the Snow

John Steinbeck
Of Mice and Men

Robert Louis Stevenson
Dr Jekyll and Mr Hyde

Jonathan Swift
Gulliver's Travels

Robert Swindells
Daz 4 Zoe

Mildred D. Taylor
Roll of Thunder, Hear My Cry

Mark Twain
Huckleberry Finn

James Watson
Talking in Whispers

Edith Wharton
Ethan Frome

William Wordsworth
Selected Poems

A Choice of Poets

Mystery Stories of the Nineteenth Century including The Signalman

Nineteenth Century Short Stories

Poetry of the First World War

Six Women Poets